BATTLING LANGUAGE RIGHTS GOVERNANCE IN AFRICA:

Swisselgianism, Ubackism, And The Ambazonia-Cameroun War

PETER ATEH-AFAC FOSSUNGU

Edited by Tendai Rinos Mwanaka

Mwanaka Media and Publishing Pvt Ltd,
Chitungwiza Zimbabwe
*
Creativity, Wisdom and Beauty

Publisher: *Mmap*
Mwanaka Media and Publishing Pvt Ltd
24 Svosve Road, Zengeza 1
Chitungwiza Zimbabwe
mwanaka@yahoo.com
mwanaka13@gmail.com
https://www.mmapublishing.org
www.africanbookscollective.com/publishers/mwanaka-media-and-publishing
https://facebook.com/MwanakaMediaAndPublishing/

Distributed in and outside N. America by African Books Collective
orders@africanbookscollective.com
www.africanbookscollective.com

ISBN: 978-1-77925-588-4
EAN: 9781779255884

© **Peter Ateh-Afac Fossungu** 2021

All rights reserved.
No part of this book may be reproduced or transmitted in any form or by any means, mechanical or electronic, including photocopying and recording, or be stored in any information storage or retrieval system, without written permission from the publisher

DISCLAIMER
All views expressed in this publication are those of the author and do not necessarily reflect the views of *Mmap*.

Dedicated To Ambazonia And All Defenders Of Human Rights

Table of Contents

Introduction..vi

Chapter 1: A Survey of Language Politics around the World with Quebec and Canada in the Witness-Box
....2

Quebec's Language Politics: Upside-down or Standing Upright?...6

Canada and United Afrika: Go for Swisselgianism Rather than for Cameroon's War-Instigating Stupidity..10

Chapter 2: Scrutinizing and Contextualizing Cameroon's Language Policy...21

Stop the Babbling on Cameroon's Language History and Go for Indonesianism...23

Cameroon and United Afrika, Indonesianism Is Saying Goodbye to Onesidetakism..27

Going for Enthusiasm and Foresight and Dropping the Dependency Syndrome..32

Debating without Understanding Debates and the African Virus of Biggytitlemania...40

Patriotically Embracing the God-given Blessings: The Nobisooh Health Centre Speech..50

Chapter 3: The Secret Agreements and Effective Bilingualism in Cameroon?..60

Cursing Cameroon's Multifaceted Blessings for Leading Africa?...61

Pre-1996 Bilingualism: The Authenticity of English and Ngoalingualism..70

Post-1996 Bilingualism: Rejecting Swisselgianism and Promotion of Indigenous Languages...76

The Great Language Puzzle and Nwangong-Zoomitionism: What is Continental in the Definition of Continent?...76

Language Lessons of Globavillagism and Closing Remarks..88

References..94

Mmap Nonfiction and Academic books........................105

INTRODUCTION

In relation to the United States of Africa that is being recommended as the sane means for Getting Africa into Africa for Africans, I am here strongly suggesting that it be styled United Democratic Afrika (UDA) – or simply United Afrika (UA) – to keep it apart from and unconfused with the USA that the Americans already firmly have in their keeping. With the prevailing and unsettling human rights situation in African countries like Cameroon, people are entitled to understand what the problem actually is and what needs to be done to permanently redress it.[1] This book in essence seeks to use the burning issue of multiculturalism (bilingualism particularly) to offer an improved grasping and appreciation of the roots and dynamics of the Ambazonia-Cameroun war that has been raging on for the past five years and still counting. Cameroon's language politics is also gainfully employed to address that of a possible UDA in the book, a contribution that is also a "revised and updated version of *some portions* of my close to 500-page 1999 doctoral dissertation at the Université de Montréal."[2] It comes to contribute toward such

---

[1] Peter Ateh-Afac Fossungu, *Getting Africa Out of the Dungeon: Human Rights, Federalism, and Judicial Politics in Cameroon* (Masvingo, Zimbabwe: Africa Talent Publishers, 2019).

[2] *Id.*, at ix (original emphasis). Also constituting parts of said doctoral research and being a significant blueprint to grasping the soul of the war in question is Peter Ateh-Afac Fossungu, *Understanding Confusion in Africa: The Politics of Multiculturalism and Nation-building in Cameroon* (Bamenda: Langaa RPCIG, 2013).

knowledge and diagnosis (if anything short of complete independence can now even make any sense to Ambazonians), in view of further providing valuable lessons in the concerned domains to United Afrika.

Of course, the book's focus is on Africa's famously infamous bilingual state called Cameroon. But the enhanced comprehension of Cameroon's language management and national unity policies that it aims at furnishing is better achieved here through a comparative survey of the language politics of four other countries: two of them European (Belgium and Switzerland), one North American (Canada), and the other Third World and Asian (Indonesia). Language politics in Cameroon obviously cannot fail to also attract attention to what prevails especially in Canada, a country from which the experts largely expect Cameroon to heavily draw and thereby begin climbing "the same flight of stairs toward the destinies reserved for us [Cameroonians and Canadians] in the world."[3] This standpoint appears to stem from the fact that Cameroon and Canada are officially plural societies linguistically, with European imperialism having enormously contributed to this state of affairs.

This critique, however, argues essentially that, for a better language governance technique that gainfully protects minorities as well as fostering the goals of national and continental unity and development, Cameroon (and, by extension, the anticipated UDA) must emulate from European countries like Belgium and Switzerland rather than from Canada which is traditionally regarded as 'the Cameroon of North America'. That the Canadian model of

---

[3] Anne F. Bayefsky, *Canada's Constitution Act 1982 and Amendments* Vol. 1 (Toronto: McGraw-Hill Ryerson, 1989) at 441.

'uniform bilingualism across the country' (or *Ubackism*) is not very much different from what is currently in operation in Cameroon and instead provoking and sustaining the ongoing war of independence. That the Swiss and Belgian formulae (styled *Swisselgianism*) do furnish better means of comfortably retaining the breaking-away Ambazonia (West Cameroon) in Cameroon as well as advancing other national-continental integration goals, not leaving out the general respect for human rights. Still in this language management domain, Indonesia is also recommended as an astute teacher in the domain of the adoption of a common African national language in Cameroon and the UDA.

There is little doubt that the "Anglophone Problem" is at the centre of state disintegration in Cameroon. A review of the mushrooming literature relating to this "Anglophone Problem"[4]

---

[4] See, for example, Fossungu, *supra*, note 2; Mufor Atanga, *The Anglophone Cameroon Predicament* (Bamenda Langaa RPCIG, 2011); Susan Dicklitch, "The Southern Cameroons and Minority Rights in Cameroon" 29(1) *Journal of Contemporary African Studies* (2011), 49-62; Emmanuel Anyefru, "Paradoxes of Internationalization of the Anglophone Problem in Cameroon" 28(1) *Journal of Contemporary African Studies* (2010), 85-101; S.E. Ebai, "The Right to Self-Determination and the Anglophone Cameroon Situation" 13(5) *The International Journal of Human Rights* (2009), 631-53; Lyonga Eko, "The English-Language Press and the 'Anglophone Problem' in Cameroon: Group Identity, Culture, and the Politics of Nostalgia" 20(1) *Journal of Third World Studies* (2003), 79-102; Piet Konings, "The Anglophone Struggle for Federalism in Cameroon", in L.R. Basita and J. Ibrahim (eds.), *Federalism and Decentralization in Africa: The Multiethnic Challenge* (Fribourg Institut du Fédéralisme, 1999), 289-325; and Piet Konings and Francis B. Nyamnjoh. "The Anglophone Problem in Cameroon" 35(2) *The Journal of Modern African Studies* (1997), 207-29.

duly exposes the burning twin issues of bijuralism (or legal dualism) and bilingualism to be stiffly responsible for the current human rights crisis and national disunity in Cameroon. Since I have already incisively and critically examined bijuralism in Cameroon elsewhere,[5] only bilingualism is specifically handled in this report that does not intend to theorize about legal bilingualism.[6] Neither does it intend to get deeply into the semantics of legal bilingualism, nor purport to be providing an epistemology of bilingualism.[7] The volume principally seeks to demonstrate the importance of a sane language policy in Africa, using Cameroon, in the protection of human rights and the promotion of national-continental unity. In the case of uniting the mini-states of Africa into a formidable political entity, official language(s) would obviously be firmly tied to ethnic/cultural origin; a plain fact that cannot be ignored in any sane language policy that has an eye fixed on national-continental unity and development.

"Although the term: Language Policy is new", William F. Mackay is said to have observed, "the practice is of great

---

[5] See Peter Ateh-Afac Fossungu, "Political Naivety, Corruption, and Poverty Promotion in Africa: Riding the 'Poorest-ugliest French' Bijuralism Horse from Cameroon to Canada via Britain", in Munyaradzi Mawere (ed.), *The Political Economy of Poverty, Vulnerability and Disaster Risk Management: Building Bridges of Resilience, Entrepreneurship and Development in Africa's 21st Century* (Bamenda: Langaa RPCIG, 2018), 123-73.

[6] As to which, instead see Roderick A. Macdonald, "Legal Bilingualism" 42 *McGill Law Journal* (1997), 119-67 at 146-57.

[7] *Id.* at 130-40 & 140-46, respectively.

antiquity"[8] since the history of thought is concerned with the history of language.[9] According to Professor Peller who wrote about "The Metaphysics of American Law" in 1985, legal thought is a representational discourse which purports to represent social relations in a neutral manner. But like language generally, legal discourse can never escape its own textuality.[10] Because language is the means to some other purpose like politics, theology, etc[11], Mackay has concluded that it is almost as old as writing, going back to the time when the English king's words first appeared on clay tablets in cuneiform characters.[12] Several experts have examined the issue and concluded that language use is indisputably ideological,[13] thus making language a very powerful tool – for better or worse – especially in the political process. This evaluation thus proposes the kind of language management strategy that

---

[8] Sunday B. Ajulo, "Myth and Reality of Law, Language and International Organization in Africa: The Case of African Economic Community" 41(1) *Journal of African Law* (1997), 27-42 at 31.

[9] M Maneli, *Perelman's New Rhetoric as Philosophy and Methodology for the Next Century* (Dordrecht: Kluwer Academic Publishers, 1994) at 26.

[10] Macdonald, *supra*, note 6 at 126.

[11] Mark Opashinov, "Book Review of Lawrence M. Solan's *The Language of Judges* University of Chicago Press (1993)" 20(2) *Queen's Law Journal* (1995), 641-47 at 641.

[12] Ajulo, *supra*, note 8 at 31.

[13] See Marc Gold, "The Mask of Objectivity: Politics and Rhetoric in the Supreme Court of Canada" 7 *Supreme Court Review* (1985), 455 at 458; Patricia J. Williams, "Alchemical Notes: Reconstructing Ideals from Deconstructed Rights" 22 *Harvard Civil Rights-Civil Liberty Law Review* (1987), 401-433 at 404-405; and L.M. Solan, *The Language of Judges* (Chicago: University of Chicago Press, 1993).

United Afrika has to adopt, doing so by exposing existing language and other cultural rights violations through a magnification of the confusion in Cameroon being called uniform bilingualism throughout the country, a misunderstanding which is mainly behind the war that was foolishly declared by President Paul Biya of La République du Cameroun (LRC) on Ambazonia. It achieves this goal through (1) surveying language politics around the world in chapter 1, which largely aids a deeper understanding of particularly (2) Cameroon's language rights provision and practice in chapters 2 and 3. There is a conclusion that harps on the imperative need for open-mindedness and vision in the domain of language rights governance.

CHAPTER 1
SURVEYING LANGUAGE POLITICS AROUND THE WORLD WITH QUEBEC AND CANADA IN THE WITNESS-BOX

All human societies without exception, we are told by Professor Northrop Frye, are enclosed in an envelope of culture, of certain social, religious, legal and other practices, and most of this cultural envelope consists of words. According to the Canadian professor, completely natural societies, if they could exist, would communicate by telepathy or some kind of body language or gestures.[14] The importance of language need not be overemphasized here. In *Attorney-General of Quebec v Les Chaussure's Brown's Inc. et al* it was held in 1988 that language is not only a means by which 'a people' may express its identity but also the means by which the individual expresses his or her personal identity and sense of individuality.[15] Researchers like Eric Anchimbe, Charles Fonchingong, and Timothy Mbuagbo have particularly furnished further readings on these vexing issues in Cameroon.[16] It has been concluded in some informed quarters

---

[14] Northrop Frye, "Language as the Home of Human Life", in Michael Owen (ed.), *Salute to Scholarship: Essays Presented at the Official Opening of Athabasca University* (Athabasca, Alberta: Athabasca University, 1986), 20-33 at 20.

[15] Mary Ellen Turpel, "Aboriginal Peoples and the Canadian Charter: Interpretive Monopolies, Cultural Differences", in R.F. Devlin (ed.), *Canadian Perspectives on Legal Theory* (Toronto: Emond Montgomery Publications Limited, 1991), 503-538 at 516.

[16] See Eric A. Anchimbe, *Language Policy and Identity Construction: The Dynamics of Cameroon's Multilingualism* (Amsterdam: John Benjamins Publishing Company, 2013); Charles

that only a people (such as Quebecers or *Southern Cameroonsians*) as a community can be integrated because, as individuals, their 'integration' can only be assimilation.[17] I have used the italicized concept of Southern Cameroonsians to argue basically that the "peoples" of British Southern Cameroons (that is now trying to break away from Cameroon to become sovereign Ambazonia) should be known as 'Southern Cameroonsians' and not as 'Southern Cameroonians' since the latter appellation has the potential of denying them the right to self-determination through confusing them for the inhabitants of the Cameroon Republic`s South Region or Province.[18] Douglas Johnson makes a similar argument for South Sudan, preferring New Sudan in place of South Sudan.[19] You see just what language improperly used can import? That is the more reason why I argue that whatever language(s) that United Afrika adopts as official/working language(s) must only be federal/continental and not necessarily imposed on individual citizens or states that would be free to use just one of the selected language(s). It may sound so complicated (especially to the dictators and other traitors) but the suggested Swisselgianism here would

---

C. Fonchingong, "Exploring the Politics of Identity and Ethnicity in State Reconstruction in 'Democratic' Cameroon'' 11(4) *Social Identities* (2005), 363-80; and Oben Timothy Mbuagbo, "Cameroon: Exploiting Anglophone Identity in State Deconstruction" 8(3) *Social Identities* (2002), 431-38.

[17] Peter C. Newman, *The Canadian Establishment* Volume 1 (Toronto: McClelland and Stewart Limited, 1968) at 297.

[18] See Fossungu, *supra*, note 2 at 40-45.

[19] See Douglas H. Johnson, "New Sudan or South Sudan? The Multiple Meanings of Self-Determination in Sudan's Comprehensive Peace Agreement" 15(2) *Civil Wars* (2013), 141-56.

considerably simplify the matter for fearful and brainwashed Africans.

Language has thus been identified by some studies on democracy in plural societies as one of the cross-cutting cleavages in Belgium and Switzerland. If this phenomenon has not yet come to the fore in Africa, experts like Lijhart have concluded, it is because a temporary solution has been found in the colonial linguistic heritage, for Africa is replete with plural societies.[20] This book finds this justification of the absence in Africa of the cross-cutting cleavages on language insufficient. The accurate answer or explanation should be that most, if not all, of these so-called independent African states are not only still dependent but are also in serious need of dedicated and patriotic leaders, for "where are the patriotism and sincerity on the part of these African leaders who are more than ready to unnecessarily spill the blood of their own citizens at the behest of a foreign power?"[21] These states are, consequently, neither democratic nor officially plural/plurilingual as most of them claim to be. Otherwise, linguistic minorities must have strong and effective community debates in them. This thesis is heavily supported by the conclusions of some Canadian experts of language politics. A minority group, some of these specialists think, must have a strong and effective community forum to advocate

---

[20] Ajulo, *supra*, note 8 at 31 n.16.

[21] Peter Ateh-Afac Fossungu, *Democracy and Human Rights in Africa: The Politics of Collective Participation and Governance in Cameroon* (Bamenda: Langaa RPCIG, 2013) at 165.

and maintain its rights, and that in this rights-protection business good leadership can make a significant difference.[22]

The leadership can obviously not be good without a sufficient grasp of the significance of language. In the presence of these conditions or qualities, (national) political leaders in multilingual polities cannot fail to pay particular attention to their language policy. For instance, the Belgian Apex Court formula of constitutional parity between the two dominant language groups quite apart,[23] we are told that former Quebec Premier Lucien Bouchard told 1,800 Péquistes (members of the Parti Québécois) in a 45-minute speech opening the party's biennial policy convention in November 1996 how "[w]e must illustrate in policies and in our programs a plan for a country that is inclusive and tolerant [because w]e are the government of all Quebecers and we will not turn our backs on a single citizen."[24] We are similarly told by President Paul Biya that "Cameroon's policy is meant to be specific and to shun ideological slavery. It is based on a collective consultation that excludes no voice."[25] Those voices, of course, ought then to be heard in the two inherited or official languages, if non-exclusion has to make sense. That is precisely what the experts think non-exclusion of any voice must connote, if it is not to be merely

---

[22] John E. Trent, "Retaking the 'Middle Ground' – Alliance Candidate Says He Offers English-speakers a Chance to Renew Group's Credibility" *Montreal Gazette* (20 March, 1999), B5.

[23] See Fossungu, *supra*, note 1 at 32-33. See also Richard Cullen, "Adaptive Federalism in Belgium" 13 *University of New South Wales Law Journal* (1990), 346-58.

[24] Cited in Fossungu, *supra*, note 2 at 64.

[25] Paul Biya, *Communal Liberalism* (London: Macmillan, 1986) at 100.

confusing and promotional of the developer theory or regression that is being now sanctioned by the ongoing senseless war in West-Central Africa. Is the claim of non-exclusion then real, for example, in Quebec, Canada, and Cameroon? Let us find out, beginning with Quebec language politics whose (un)holy bible is Bill 101.[26]

Language Politics in Quebec: Upside-down or Standing Upright?

Different people would give different responses to the quiz here. For instance, to the standing upright option, one commentator says, in the presence of Bill 101, "I don't think so."[27] This is because "[t]he orthodoxy of language in Quebec", according to Editor Alan Allnutt,

means that no provincial opposition leader can effectively speak out against any part of the law [called Bill 101]. It means that federal cabinet ministers from Quebec must smile through clenched teeth and extol the virtues of a discriminatory law. And most provincial leaders outside Quebec have been brain-washed to believe that any questioning of the law's virtues will lead to chaos and the end of Canada within days.[28]

Allnutt is not alone. Other commentators think it is a whole paradox in Canada, having led a critic of Cameroon's 'intellectual

---

[26] See *Charter of the French Language*, R.S.Q., ch. 11 (1977) (Can) (hereinafter Bill 101).

[27] Alan Allnutt, "Challenging the Orthodoxy of Bill 101" *Montreal Gazette* (20 March 1999), B5.

[28] *Ibid.*

paradoxes' to kind of kill two French 'orthodoxical birds' with just one stone. I am particularly referring to the language rights critic who pondered why Cameroon's minister of Higher Education who is Anglophone refused to speak English in Montreal: wondering whether the minister could just have been trying not to offend Quebec's own paradox of 'only French in Quebec' when the province is part and parcel of an officially/constitutionally, de jure and de facto bilingual Canada.[29]

Talking of the *Montreal Gazette*, in critiquing Jennifer Robinson's column in the *Montreal Gazette* (of Tuesday, 4 December 1998) that posited that it is not just the separation issue that discourages Anglophones from voting for the Parti Quebecois and that there is a long litany of reasons in addition to separation, Tony Kondaks also wrote to the *Montreal Gazette* from Mesa, Arizona in the USA, as follows:

> Now it is most certainly true that the reasons she gives are things that [Quebec] anglos hate. What Ms. Robinson fails

---

[29] "Or would the minister just have been trying not to offend Quebec's own paradox of 'only French in Quebec' when that province is part and parcel of an officially/constitutionally, de jure and de facto bilingual Canada? I will not delve into this Quebec issue here. *The Montréal Gazette* (which some diehard Quebec separatists would have instructed us during *Sunday Edition* of February 2, 1997 not to over read) is always carrying a lot of discussion regarding it. I need only add that such paradoxes have plainly become the rule rather than the exception in Cameroon principally because Cameroonians have come to over believe in mirages called 'intellectuals' or those with so-called 'Higher Education'." Peter Ateh-Afac Fossungu, "Paradoxes of Cameroon's Intellectuals" *The Herald* (Yaoundé, 16-18 January 1998), 4.

to tell your readers is that, with very few exceptions, the Liberal Party of Quebec is as guilty of these infractions, if not more. Specifically:
- Promoting the interests and rights of francophones.
- Promoting French-ethnic nationalism by portraying the English presence in Quebec as a threat.
- Restricting access to English schools.
- Having a long tradition of inward-looking, exclusionist policies that overlook the contribution that non-francophones have made and continue to make to Quebec.
- Showing open hostility toward English community leaders.[30]

On the above points, according to Tony Kondaks, the Liberal Party of Quebec has a demonstrated record of being as bad as or worse than the PQ. As for senior jobs for Anglophone Quebecer, access to health and social services, and language police, he affirms, "the Liberal record is a wee bit better than the PQ's – but not that much better."[31] Conspicuously absent from Ms. Robinson's list of complaints, as kondaks pursued, were:

- Having only French as an official language of Quebec.

- Implementing the francization provisions of Bill 101 (obvious violation of freedom of speech and freedom of association).

---

[30] Tony Kondaks, "Liberals Were as Bad for Anglos as the PQ" *Montreal Gazette* (15 December 1998), B2.
[31] *Ibid.*

- Disgustingly low (less than one per cent) representation of anglos in the civil service. (Why Ms. Robinson seems to be more concerned with elites getting senior jobs in government, as she mentions in her piece, more than the regular guy in the civil service I can't understand).[32]

Professor William Green also discusses the violation of freedom of speech and of freedom of association by Bill 101.[33] As the language rights critic from Arizona concluded his letter to the editor, "On the above three points, again, the Liberal record is as bad as or worse than the PQ."[34] This may thus explain why the Quebec Premier had to tell his ruling PQ that "[t]he most important test and one which is the most arduous is our linguistic policy" wherein "[w]e have [to succeed] to be the government that will have proven to Quebecers it can manage a country."[35] Has Canada itself succeeded to be the country that would have proven to Quebec that the latter can safely remain within Canada? The same query applies, of course, with greater force to Cameroon with what is now known as Ambazonia; as well as to *prospective joiners* of the UDA. This is where crisebacologists (or balanced critical thinkers) think Canada (like Cameroon and the UDA) would need

---

[32] *Ibid.*

[33] See William Green, "Schools, Signs, and Separation: Quebec Anglophones, Canadian Constitutional Politics, and International Language Rights" 27 *Denver Journal of International Law and Policy* (1999), 449 at 469-73.

[34] Kondaks, *supra*, note 30.

[35] Philip Authier, "Bouchard Calls for Tolerance: Economy First" *Montreal Gazette* (23 November 1996), A1 at A1 & A11, respectively.

to go to Belgium and Switzerland (and not to Cameroon) to learn how that minority language rights protection business is correctly done.

Canada and United Afrika: Go for Open Swisselgianism, Not for Cameroon's War-Instigating Stupidity

The experts think the Belgian and Swiss Strict Territorial Principles (STPs) could be very helpful to Canada in its desire to keep Quebec within the country and to Cameroon for avoiding the breakaway of Ambazonia. This territorial principle or *Swisselgianism* is exactly what Canada seems to be adhering to, albeit in a very questionable 'roundaboutist' and dangerously 'advanced' manner; thus making Canada what some keen observers have dubbed a *Hypocracy*[36] which is in order to distinguish it, at least, from what some see as Cameroon's stupidity called *Advanced Democracy*.[37] A Canadian scholar living and working in Switzerland has provided an insightful discussion of the differences in the Swiss and Canadian federal systems. André Liebich of the Graduate Institute of International Studies in Geneva tends to suggest that there is much in the Swiss formula that Cameroon (standing in for the UDA) and Canada have to emulate. He begins by posing questions as to what the Swiss might know that Canadians and Cameroonians don't; and

---

[36] See Peter Ateh-Afac Fossungu, *Africans and Negative Competition in Canadian Factories: Revamping Canada's Immigration, Employment and Welfare Policies?* (Bamenda: Langaa RPCIG, 2015) at 133-38 & 114-22.

[37] Fossungu, *supra*, note 21 at 65.

whether the Swiss example can be transplanted to Canadian and African soil. He is pushed to ask these questions largely because:

> Instead of bringing the country to the brink of dissolution [like almost happened in Canada in 1995], Switzerland's linguistic communities [a dominant German-speaking majority and French-speaking minority known as Romands] – including a small Italian community (four percent of the population) and a very small but recognized fourth one (one percent Romansch) – cooperate in apparent harmony.[38]

While admitting that the Swiss federal formula for linguistic coexistence is not easily transferable 'like a plant', it may be important for others similarly placed to recognize that the success there could result principally from the fact that Switzerland, like Belgium, follows the language STP. "Switzerland is run on a strictly territorial principle: you and your children are expected to speak the language of the area which you happen to live in. If that is not agreeable, your only option is to move."[39] Since 1970, Belgium has four language Regions: the unilingual Dutch, French and German and the bilingual (Dutch and French) Brussels regions.[40] The Swiss

---

[38] André Liebich, "Federalism Swiss Style" *McGill News* (Alumni Quarterly, Spring 1996), 11 at 11.

[39] *Id.* at 12. J. Rohr's two books provide more details on this Swiss style: *La démocratie en Suisse* (Economica, 1987) & *La Suisse contemporaine: société et sa politique* (Clin, 1972).

[40] See Evan Joel Shapiro, *The Supranational Challenge: Federal and Decentralized Unitary States Within the European Union* (LL.M. Thesis, McGill University, 1995) at 99.

federal formula in particular is one of the feasible forms of 'encouraging bilingualism' in Cameroon – if Cameroon's Article 1(3) of the 1996 Constitution[41] that is more extensively discussed in Chapter 3, is anything to go by. With this Swiss formula, it would not be proper for a national official to appear in a language-zone and speak a language other than that territory's own. As a language rights advocate, I forcefully put the vexing bilingualism and secession questions in Cameroon in a way in 1998 when I pondered:

> Where do Anglophones in this country think they are heading for? For their own Second Home? And do they know what that Second Home of theirs could be like? As I see it, all this Second Home talk is nonsensical and might only show how stupid most of us in this country are. I explain. Let us go back in time to a decade or so. Just a few months after having unilaterally changed 'Victoria' in the South West Province and deleted 'United' from this country's name in February 1984, the current president would go to Bamenda in the North-West Province – the other of the two 'Anglophone provinces' – and very haltingly make this simple phrase that many critics say he must have been rehearsing for close to five months: 'Bamenda is my second home'....[42]

---

[41] See *Loi N° 96-06 du 18 janvier 1996 portant révision de la Constitution du 02 juin 1972* [hereinafter 1996 Constitution].

[42] Peter Ateh-Afac Fossungu, "Revisiting 'My Second Home'" *The Herald* N° 652 (26-27 August 1998), 10.

The problem I had here extends to the fact that, rather than question to know where the president's 'first home' was, Anglophones sonorously clapped for him for that useless and divisive sentence in a long French speech![43] As the critic in me then explained that declaration off, "the 'Second Fiddle Syndrome' in this and other examples is clear enough. And that is precisely how the state is guaranteeing the promotion of bilingualism throughout the country? This particular example does not only divide Anglophones and Francophones; it also fortifies their solidly placed wedge between the two [English-speaking] provinces: if Francophone Cameroon is the *first*, North West Anglophone Cameroon is *second*, and, of course, South West Anglophone Cameroon is third (or not even among?)"[44] President Biya was (as any future leader of the UDA) normally supposed to address the people there in English entirely, if bilingualism is the norm in Cameroon. After all (assuming that the UDA adopts the following six African languages as its official languages: Arabic, Bambara, Lingala, Swahili, Yoruba, and Zulu[45]), as Canada itself is quite aware of (as exposed in its 1967 Royal Commission Report), a bilingual (or multilingual) country is not one in which all the

---

[43] *Ibid.* See also Aloysius Ngefac, "Linguistic Choices in Postcolonial Multilingual Cameroon" 19(3) *Nordic Journal of African Studies* (2010), 149-64.

[44] Fossungu, *supra*, note 42 (original emphasis).

[45] I am not unaware that most people would rather be favouring the OAU language-choices of Arabic, English, French, Portuguese, and Spanish. You can still substitute them in the demonstration here; but see the discussion on the Babbling on Cameroon's Language History, including Common Indigenous Language Choice below in chapter 2.

inhabitants must necessarily speak the two (or all the) official languages. It is rather a country where the principal institutions, both public and private, must serve the public in both (or all the) languages. This means that the majority of the members of the public can be unilingual.[46] Applying Swisselgianism, therefore, it means that any *Afrikan* (to distinguish from citizens of the African mini-states not in the UDA) moving to take up residence in the UDA state of Kenya, for instance, must be ready to speak Swahili there. If that is not agreeable, his or her only option is to move! Can you not begin to see just how multilingual Afrikans would very voluntarily become from Swisselgianism? Is it not straightforwardly better than Canada's hypocrisy?

Could Cameroon have actually accomplished its famous boasting in the *denrée* exportation business by having successfully exported its foolish brand of bilingualism to Canada[47]? To come down squarely on this imported 'advanced' strategy to Canada, it is helpful to realize that Canada's *Ubackism* or 'Uniform Bilingualism across the Country (UBAC)' – that is entrenched in the 1982 *Charter*[48] and which firmly and loudly would be saying NO to Swisselgianism – has been

---

[46] Cited in Jacques Benjamin, *Les camerounais occidentaux: la minorité dans un état bicommunautaire* (Montréal: Université de Montréal, 1972) at 197 n.2. See also George Etchu and Allan W. Grundstorm, *Official Bilingualism and Linguistic Communication in Cameroon-Bilinguisme officiel et communication linguistique au Cameroun* (New York: P. Lang, 1999).

[47] See Fossungu, *supra*, note 21 at xv; & Fossungu, *supra*, note 5 at 144-51.

[48] See *The Canadian Charter of Rights and Freedoms*, Part I of the *Constitution Act, 1982*, being Schedule B to the *Canada Act 1982* (U.K.), 1982, c.11.

seen as a means of national unity, a way of formally binding French and English Canada into a single political entity by such means as making English and French language rights uniform across the country. The inclusion of mobility rights in the *Charter* was an additional attempt to avoid the balkanization of Canada and advance national unity by affording individuals the right to live and work in the province of their choosing 'without discrimination based on the previous province of residence'.[49]

To emphasize and explain why United Afrika's real national-continental unity need is Swisselgianism and not Ubackism, the question would thus become that of knowing if Quebec's Bill 101 is a justified exception to Canada's uniformity in language rights across the country? In other words, is Bill 101 paradoxical on Quebec's part or on Canada's part? At first sight, Bill 101 is a paradox on the part of Quebec (as most of the critical literature above is portraying). However, on a closer crisebacological look and examination of 'the practice of legal bilingualism in Canada,'[50] it is in fact only a paradox on the part of Canada. It is my thought that the seemingly insoluble language and separation tussle continues to rock Canada (including Quebec) simply because Canada (excluding Quebec) has come to over believe in mirages called UBAC or 'uniform bilingualism across the country'. The hiding of the Canadian mirage is almost similar to camouflaging

---

[49] Frank Iacobucci, "Judicial Review by the Supreme Court of Canada under the Charter of Rights and Freedoms: The First Ten Years", in David M. Beatty (ed.), *Human Rights and Judicial Review – A Comparative Perspective* (Dordrecht: Martinus Nijhoff Publishers, 1994), 93-134 at 94-95.

[50] See Macdonald, *supra*, note 6 at 157-65; and Green, *supra*, note 33 at 453-61.

assimilation in Cameroon, with the sole difference just being Quebec's status as a province in a federation proper. It is principally because Quebecers (very unlike 'Anglo-Cameroonsians') have long stiffly refused to be easily fooled by this 'Kontchoumeterized' or 'Advanced' bilingualism which is nicely clothed in Ubackism that Canada remains what a political science professor at the University of Toronto calls a Constitutional Odyssey.[51] *Kontchoumeterized* is a Cameroonian synonym for 'deceitful' and crisebacologists are inclined to think that Quebec is plainly telling 'the Rest of Canada' to be honest enough to openly accept the Swisselgian territorial language principle throughout Canada (not excepting Quebec). Doing so clearly means that Canada must end its Cameroon-inspired *Ngoa-lingualism*, which means 'unilingualism under the camouflage of bilingualism throughout the country.'[52]

The Ngoa-lingualism accusation from Quebec is the plain fact, with the Province's views being fortified by even a fleeting look at Donald Rowat's 'Governing Federal Capitals'.[53] It is only too well known, according to Professor Jacques Benjamin of the Université de Montréal, that such capitals do reflect the real status of linguistic minorities in officially plurilingual states.[54] It is (if there was in fact

---

[51] See Peter H. Russell, *Constitutional Odyssey: Can Canadians Become a Sovereign People?* 3rd edition (Toronto: University of Toronto Press, 2004).

[52] Fossungu, *supra*, note 2 at 172.

[53] See Donald C. Rowat, "The Problems of Governing Federal Capitals" 1(3) *Revue canadienne de science politique* (septembre 1968), 345-56

[54] "*Le statu réel de la minorité linguistique dans un Etat officiellement bilingue est révélé, entre autres, par les facilités que*

any federation in Cameroon) also well known, according to the Joint Declaration of the Prime Ministers of Canada, of Quebec, and of Ontario on 1 February 1968 in *The Ottawa Journal*, that "[t]he capital region of [a veritable federation such as the recommended UDA and] Canada should be so constituted and developed to reflect fully the linguistic and cultural values of the two [or many] founding peoples and thus encourage in all Canadians [and Afrikans] a feeling of pride and participation in, and attachment to their capital."[55] Is this actually what was/is in Canada and Cameroon? Let us leave Cameroon's case for a later scrutiny in the next two chapters and quickly wrap up with Canada's awkwardness called Ubackism. By not openly embracing Swisselgianism, Canada remains a big joke or contradiction (a *Hypocracy* as some critics like to call it), especially as it does not (like the USA and Nigeria) have a distinct Federal Capital Territory. Just don't be fooled by the Ottawa-Gatineau mirage. "Ottawa francophones", as we are plainly told by a political columnist at *Le Soleil* in Quebec City,

would doubtless be happy to receive municipal services in French equivalent to those available in English in Montreal even if

---

la capitale fédérale lui accorde. Les droits des francophones de s'exprimer dans leur langue lorsqu'ils se rendent à Ottawa et à Berne, et ceux des Flamands à Bruxelles, ont été reconnues ces dernières années, non sans difficultés parfois." Benjamin, *supra*, note 46 at 125.

[55] *Id* at 198 n.8. "*Il s'agira [aussi] de voir comment on conçoit au Cameroun l'usage et protection de la langue officielle de la minorité en particulier dans la capitale fédérale et a l'Université fédérale, et d'insister ensuite sur l'une des causes de cet unilinguisme de fait de la langue française, celle de la présence de la France au Cameroun, si nécessaire par ailleurs au développement du pays*" *Id*.at 123.

Montreal is not officially recognized as a bilingual city. However, it is highly doubtful that they would get such services in Ottawa even with legally recognized bilingual status. Even less so without this law. Just go to Nepean or to Kanata to confirm that.[56]

Although Canada's *Charter* guarantees freedom of expression (including linguistic expression) in Section 2(b) and pledges bilingual rights in federal parliamentary and judicial proceedings with the federal government in Sections 17-20, there is no guarantee of UBAC: so long as the 1867 *British North America Act*'s Section 93 has not been abolished or overridden by the 1982 *Charter* (as it clearly has not nullified it). This Section 93 permits provincial legislatures to 'exclusively make laws in relation to education' including the language of instruction.[57] Canada's 1867 *Constitution Act* (otherwise known as the *British North America Act*), it must be reiterated, while remaining "the basic element of Canada's written constitution", is, however, "not the whole and even with the addition of the *Constitution Act, 1982* is only the skeleton of the set of arrangements by which Canadians are governed."[58] Thus, in the awkward constitutional scenario created, it is Quebec alone that finds itself between the hammer and anvil. I think a lot of people are wont to just jump into critiquing Quebec language politics without really grasping the essential dynamics at work, most probably because they are not detached and objective. Objectivity

---

[56] Michel David, "Francophones Outside Quebec Pose Problem" *Montreal Gazette* (10 December 1999), B3 (altered paragraphing).

[57] See Green, *supra*, note 33 at 453 & 454.

[58] Eugene Forsey, *How Canadians Govern Themselves* (2nd edition, 1988), in G.P. Van Nes, *The Structure of Federalism* (1989), 7.

and vision are primary to any successful dialoguing relating to the UDA creation, as harped upon in Chapter 2. Thus, as some language rights critics have put the Quebec point succinctly,

Whenever the rights of francophones outside Quebec are threatened, the Quebec government finds itself squeezed between the moral obligation to fly to their assistance and that of defending Quebec's own linguistic security [because] As shocking as Ontario's indifference to Ottawa francophones may be, Quebec cannot afford to push too much without agreeing that [then Ontario Premier] Mike Harris can come along and demand easier access to English schools or more bilingualism in Quebec hospitals.[59]

That would certainly not be the case if Swisselgianism was openly the rule in Canada. My sane suggestion to Canada (which a revamped Cameroon/UDA must not emulate in this wise until the former heeds to this recommendation) then is this. Keep Section 93 of the *B.N.A. Act* but openly apply the Swisselgian Formula throughout Canada (not excepting Quebec) and be sure that Quebec will be more comfortable in Canada and the seemingly interminable separation or secession talk could be out of the picture. That is what seems to be the possible solution. Otherwise, there is practically no difference in Canada's Ubackism and Cameroon's fraudulent version of *bilinguisme géographique* which is synonymous to its 'Poorest-ugliest French' bijuralism.[60] Many Cameroonians interviewed by an expert in 1972 brandished this concept of '*bilinguisme géographique*' (geographical bilingualism) to explain why English is the official language West of the Mungo River but certainly not in the capital of the federated state of East

---

[59] David, *supra*, note 56.
[60] Fossungu, *supra*, note 5.

Cameroon ('*et certainement pas dans la capital de l'État fédéré francophone*'[61]). But was Yaoundé not then also the capital of (federal) Cameroon? As some people would be quick to say, that was then. But what is actually the language and politics situation now in Cameroon, Africa's supposed pathfinder?

---

[61] Benjamin, *supra*, note 46 at 126.

CHAPTER 2
SCRUTINIZING AND CONTEXTUALIZING CAMEROON'S LANGUAGE POLICY

The foregoing exposition of language policies was largely from a part of the so-called First World with two or more main languages and cultures. But it does not have to end there and Cameroon cannot convincingly hide behind its "Third World" status that has too often been used by Western literature to unnecessarily justify authoritarian rule in that World. No common language, history, and this and that. Poverty, ethnicity, illiteracy, and.... (the list is endless). Like many others, I have also catalogued and critiqued some of these excuses.[62] Cameroon's policy book advances its 'language tower of Babel' excuses for the dictatorship called Advanced Democracy, further claiming, for instance, that:

> the different quarters of our towns at times show signs of ethnic peculiarities which, in such a particularly explosive spatial concentration, recall the human contradictions of our society.... Our religious divisions themselves are no less sources of social conflict. In this context and in spite of what has been achieved in promoting unity, the demons of tribalism still remain a permanent and serious threat to the stability of our institutions.[63]

---

[62] See Fossungu, *supra*, note 2 at 111-113; and John Mokum Mbaku, *Protecting Minority Rights in African Countries: A Constitutional Political Economy Approach* (Cheltenham, UK: Edward Elgar Publishing Ltd., 2018).

[63] Biya, *supra*, note 25 at 31.

This justification evokes the same theory that is synonymous to that of the Anglophone Minister of 'Higher Education' who obdurately refused to *unfrancophonize* even in bilingual Canada. Don't these so-called elites similarly refuse to Africanize even in Africa? Bashing the demons of tribalism while refusing to give them what they need for unbecoming the demons. Their entire approach is recommended reading not only for traitor studies but also for anyone who cares about both genuine intellectualism and multiculturalism in Cameroon or Africa. As already mentioned, said obstacles, according to some experts like Professor Neal Riemer of Drew University (USA), "help to explain why many of the new states have often moved away from liberal or even democratic socialist ideas and toward rule by a strong charismatic leader, a single party, a disciplined military junta, and even (often reluctantly) toward authoritarian methods in order to foster primary national values."[64] It is the belief of balanced critical thinkers that the validity or otherwise of these general statements about Third World leaders has only to be tested in the individual cases. This means that we cannot grasp their veracity in regard of Cameroon until we understand, among other things, the real meaning to be attached to the 'real Language Tower of Babel'[65] that Cameroon is said to be. Professor Mohr of Osgoode Hall Law School thinks he has this real connotation. As the professor has cautioned, we may well begin in the safety of listening to differ*a*nce because, 'Babel', as grounded in a text and tradition, has an ontology, a phenomenology, and an epistemology (albeit negative) which are

---

[64] Cited in Fossungu, *supra*, note 2 at 112.
[65] Biya, *supra*, note 25 at 31.

suspended in the kinds of 'babbles' that would be exemplified in Genesis 11:7 (that is, the invitation to go down there and confuse their language so that they may not understand each other).[66] Cameroon, the experts think, is actually a real language babbling tower and not a real language tower of Babel. What do the crisebaclogists have to tender as explanation?

Stop the Babbling on Cameroon's Language History and Go for Indonesianism

They advance the genuineness of patriotism and charisma revolving around two considerations: (1) the issue of common history and language (in this Chapter), and (2) that of whether there could be effective bilingualism for Cameroon as claimed by its latest 1996 Constitution (in Chapter 3). The crisebacologists' babbling thesis takes roots from this important passage from an expert of political integration in fragmentary societies. Professor Willard Johnson stated as far back as 1970 that:

> Cameroon has been a meeting ground of diverse cultures throughout recorded history. Its more than 150 distinct peoples make it the most pluralistic of indigenous African societies. All the European influences Africa has known have affected these traditional cultures, some of them profoundly. Portuguese, Spanish, and Dutch trading

---

[66] J.W. Mohr, "From Saussure to Derida: Margins of Law" 18 *Queen's Law Journal* (1993), 343-79 at 344 n.1. A more extensive discussion of this concept of Babel is furnished by Macdonald, *supra*, note 6 at 121-24; and C.M.B. Bram, "The Terminology of Babel: A Suggestion" 19(2) *Journal of West African Languages* (1989), 125-27.

companies operated important stations in the area 250 years before the missionaries set up permanent posts in the mid-19th century. *The only previous experience these peoples had had with common political rule was that provided by the Germans which began in 1884 and lasted until French and English forces began to drive the Germans out in 1914 [and divided] the old German colony of Kamerun between [themselves].*[67]

There is a lot that can be said about this passage in regard of the babbling in Cameroon but this work will limit itself to just two principle and interconnected issues: common history and common language. Several dedicated and patriotic leaders of the Third World have not failed to use history and language positively in the political advancement of their people and country. If there can be any claim to patriotism in Cameroon that is not to be simply offensive, then one would think the emphasized portion of the above passage (which is also directed to those corner-kickers propagating the 'myth' that Cameroonians lack common history or historical sense of belonging) is what should have been forcefully emphasized to Cameroonians. Effectively resurrecting this common history for purposes of national unity and development will be the kind of rhetoric known as 'popular rhetoric' or what Bryant has termed "oratorical falsification to hide meaning."[68] Some others consider

---

[67] Willard R. Johnson, *The Cameroon Federation: Political Integration in a Fragmentary Society* (Princeton, N.J.: Princeton University Press, 1970) at xiii (emphasis added).

[68] Gold, *supra*, note 13 at 457.

it to be "simply wrong and very often ... self-deludingly disingenuous."[69]

But crisebacologists will make bold and assert that doing this is not always bad since rhetoric of its very nature is commonplace in the history of imagined communities (like the USA, Canada, and Australia) that have evolved into nations.[70] Resurrecting old wisdom from oblivion and presenting it in light of new conflicts and antagonisms usually constitutes an innovation and a significant step forward.[71] Thus, two Chinese proverbs ('to study the old to understand the new' and 'to know from antiquity to explain the present') have also been cited to "amply testify to the traditional belief that history is a mirror reflecting the present, a source of light serving as a guide to the present age."[72] That is precisely why the tradition of Malawi unity in ancient times has lately been called in aid by modern Malawian nationalists as a powerful emotive influence for the building of a modern state.[73] Was Africa not different from what it is today before the 1884 Berlin Conference that indiscriminately parcelled it out without our input or consultation? Why wouldn't that history also be called in aid now as a commanding emotional pressure for the building of the UDA?

---

[69] Opashinov, *supra*, note 11 at 643 (omission supplied).

[70] Richard Bjornson, *The African Quest for Freedom and Identity: Cameroonian Writing and the National Experience* (Bloomington & Indianapolis: Indiana University Press, 1991) at 109.

[71] Maneli, *supra*, note 9 at 2 & 17.

[72] Daikasu Ikeda, *A Lasting Peace* Vol. II (New York & Tokyo: Weatherhill, 1987) at 187.

[73] Basil Davidson, *Africa in History: Themes and Outlines* rev. & exp. ed. (New York: Macmillan, 1991) at 165.

'Popular rhetoric' then is only to be deplored when (as is glaringly the case in Cameroon) it is rampantly manipulated by a government that exercises arbitrary authority over its citizens since, in this instance, "it contains an implicit threat against anyone who questions the official truth."[74] These implicit threat and official truth have always been commanding that Cameroon must be and remain the Advanced Dictatorial State that it is because it is not only a meeting ground of diverse foreign cultures that couple with the over 150 distinct local ones, but also because the over three hundred indigenous Cameroonian languages clearly exclude 'Western' Democracy. This is the truth that only comes from the authorities, according to Cameroon's crazy 'democracy' – *La vérité vient d'en haut...* (so that anything not coming from 'la-haut' merely becomes rumour) ...*et la rumeur vient d'en bas.*[75] Professor Maneli has strongly refuted the Encyclopaedia of Diderot's claim that there is only one road to truth – by convincingly demonstrating how there are many roads leading to truth.[76] Dias also cites William Falkner on 'truth' to the effect that no one individual can look at the truth intact.[77] Ian Robertson adds more flesh to the issue by emphasizing that "the world does not consist of a reality that everyone sees in exactly the same way. A house may seem to be simply a house, but different people will look at it and interpret it

---

[74] Bjornson, *supra*, note 70 at 109. See also Fossungu, *supra*, note 21 at 63-66.

[75] Cited in Fossungu, *supra*, note 2 at 1-2.

[76] Maneli, *supra*, note 9 at 3 & 9.

[77] R.W.M. Dias, *Jurisprudence* 4th edition (London: Butterworth, 1976) at Preface.

quite differently"[78] While these experts are handling the general falsity of Cameroon's truth theory, crisebacologists will instead be expecting me to continue analyzing Cameroon's *la-haut* language policy from its pretending patriots.[79]

Cameroon and United Afrika, Indonesianism Is Saying Goodbye to Onesidetakism

Professor Sunday Ajulo provides a smart survey of what has been called 'co-lingualism' in African countries such as Uganda, Tanzania, and Nigeria; also furnishing the distinction between their 'working' and 'official' languages.[80] Nothing of the sort exists in Cameroon. There is no indigenous language that co-exists with the 'inherited languages' either as official or working languages. These are important matters that the UDA must have to carefully grapple with. It is amazing that Cameroon, to this very moment, is still hiding behind the absence of a common national working/official language: despite the fact that "Cameroonian linguists have counted

---

[78] Ian Robertson, *Sociology* 3rd edition (New York: Worth Publishers, 1987) at 4.

[79] As Barry Fohtung has duly exposed, "For 34 years in some of the highest offices in this land, 13 [now 39] at the helm of state, and for all the experience usually – and often wrongly – associated with longevity of service, for all his claim to patriotism for his people, Mr. Biya's dreams and aspirations for his people, his most precious gift to them, have been summarised in the 60 articles of the draft constitution tabled before parliament last week [which, of course, became the 69-article 1996 Constitution barely one month later]." Cited in Fossungu, *supra*, note 21 at 51 (original square brackets).

[80] *Supra*, note 8 at 32 & 30-31, respectively.

two hundred and thirty-six [indigenous Cameroonian] languages of which *about one hundred can be standardized.*[81] Indeed, proven research efforts have also shown that it is feasible to teach any subject, including the law, in the indigenous languages of sub-Saharan Africa. As B. Rwezara, for instance, has succeeded in using Kiswahili as the language of law in Tanzania, it shows without doubt that, if the necessary political will could be mustered, other African countries should succeed in similar linguistic enterprises.[82] Is it not so shameful that none of the Cameroonian languages in question is today national after more than sixty years of 'independence'? "What a frightening truth," writes Aldarin Ngwafor, "to accept that after [more than] 37 years of independence, our learned authorities have narcotized this idea despite their brilliant academic race in renowned universities abroad. Is it fright to start, fright to fail or ignorance?"[83] This pertinent language-adoption question from the youths cannot fail to drag in the entire newspaper piece relating to our notorious Anglophone 'Higher Education' minister who studied in the USA. In a conference with his compatriots held at the Université de Montréal, Cameroon's Higher Education minister is said to have

---

[81] Biya, *supra*, note 25 at 104 (emphasis added).

[82] Ajulo, *supra*, note 8 at 33; also see the copious texts cited and discussed in Harry Kuchah Kuchah, "Early English Medium Instruction in Francophone Cameroon: The Injustice of Equal Opportunity" @ www.academia.edu/34773512/Kuchah_Kuchah_2017_Early_English_medium_instruction_in_Francophone_Cameroon_Pre_publication_version (accessed 27 November 2018).

[83] Aldarin Ngwafor, "Urgent Need for a Law School in Cameroon" *The Herald* (Yaoundé, 12-14 June 1998), 4.

puzzled right-thinking English-speaking members of his audience. Said report would indicate, for instance, that:

For illustration, take the meeting of President Biya's former Honourable Higher Education Minister – himself an Anglophone – on Sunday, September 22, 1998 with Cameroonians in Montreal, held at the *Université de Montréal*. An inquirer at that *Montréal Rencontre* had to cut the Higher Education Minister's 'Anglo-castigating' speech and inquired specifically about "The 'Anglo-Saxon' University of Buea" as the decree itself that created it is said to call it.... "*Le Cameroun de demain*," Minister Peter Agbor Tabi had also hastily cut in (apparently uneasy with being dragged to speak a language that does not sell in the circle to which he would now appear to belong), "*c'est pour les gens comme moi*...." Is Anglo-Saxonism not now a misnomer in Cameroon?

Whatever the case, it would be unnecessary here to go into all the ranting of the minister's that then followed, except to hold it up as being truly indicative of what has become of the Anglophone in Cameroon. Had any of you been there at that *Montréal Rencontre*, as a sensible Anglophone, you would have been ashamed (not of yourself though, but) of this rootless, vainly boastful individual who, given the chance, would not even attempt finding the manipulated and/or lost roots. And, to be sure, that shame of yours would simply have turned into pity at the point that the minister would even call on Anglophones to thank President Paul Biya for appointing an Anglophone (himself!) as minister of that ministerial department

And, furthermore, being the proud Anglophone Cameroonian that you could think you are, the minister's poor '*quartier*-like' French must have extremely bored your ears. And that being the case, you would not have failed to ponder aloud whether the sporadic bursts of laughter from the French-speaking members of that audience were tied to what was being said or to the quality of the language it was coming through. And, finally, you must have really wondered what on earth stopped the minister from talking in the foreign language that he was more comfortable in. And the more especially so as he was in Canada?[84]

Just substitute 'Anglophone' with 'African' in the passage for readers to amply see this same savagely un-African demeanour too with rootless administrators (like those of Alou Sub-Division in Lebialem Division, as seen below) trampling on tradition and customs in just whatever manner they chose to. People with Higher Education indeed! Are these really people who can ever think about African liberation, talk less of promoting and achieving it? That necessarily also drags in "the million dollar question: *Are Lessons in Four-Eyesism Really What Africa Really Needs for Its Liberation, Protection and Development?* That is, a necessity for properly *Getting Africa into Africa?*"[85] Traitors to their own community! Just as much a deception as the African Union (AU) stuff eh? Do the Foumban 'intellectuals in politics' have any answers to give to these inquisitive youths? Who are these 'intellectuals'? Is the staggering non-existence of a common indigenous language in Cameroon (that is littered with 'intellectuals in politics') actually due to fright to start, fright to fail or simply ignorance?

---

[84] Fossungu, *supra*, note 28.

[85] Peter Ateh-Afac Fossungu, *Family Law and Politics with Biology and Royalty in Africa and North America* (Chitungwiza, Zimbabwe: Mwanaka Media and Publishing, 2021) at 117.

In his "African Languages and National Development" (Paper delivered at a Seminar on the Teaching of African Languages in African Universities, held on 20-24 July 1987 at the University of Lagos) Bangbose sternly condemned the "neglect of African languages in national development."[86] The monumental shame in all this "neglect of African languages in national development" in Cameroon is even magnified when one comes to think of the joint communiqué from the Foumban Conference in 1961 which was conspicuously read to the press by Honourable John Ngu Foncha (then West Cameroon Prime Minister and leader of the western or Anglophone delegation) whose "keen interest in the unity of the nation and preservation of its democratic institutions" has been noticeably lauded by Dr HNA Enonchong.[87] The said communiqué branded the two official languages (English and French) as 'imported', stressing that they were to be replaced by an indigenous language and culture.[88] What has since become of this replacement? Has Cameroon not as yet had the time and opportunity to be transformed into a Shining Star for Africa to follow?

In answering an associated question ('How realistic is the OAU Language Policy?'[89] an expert has asserted that "to the extent that the framers of the Charter thought of using African languages at a future date and gave them pride of place before English and French in the document, they could be said to have

---

[86] Ajulo, *supra*, note 8 at 36.
[87] See Fossungu, *supra*, note 2 at 65.
[88] See Benjamin, *supra*, note 46 at 124.
[89] Ajulo, *supra*, note 8 at 36-37.

established a high degree of patriotism."⁹⁰ But they were probably also not serious about the matter since until now "the actual use of African languages in national economic development is [still] bedeviled by the colonial heritage."⁹¹ The Foumban actors in 'Miniature Africa' are no less guilty of the charges since nothing has happened in the direction despite all the recent rhetoric in Cameroon's 1998 Education Law about "ensur[ing] the constant adaptation of the educational system to national economic and socio-cultural realities, and also to the international environment, especially through the promotion of bilingualism and the teaching of national languages."⁹² When then is that Foumban-declared replacement of foreign languages by indigenous one(s) coming? What is the indigenous language(s) to be chosen?

Going for Enthusiasm and Foresight and Dropping the Dependency Syndrome

We are told by the experts that when Cameroon's President Amadou Ahidjo even flirted with the idea, he foresaw no other language to be used than his 'Fulfulde'.⁹³ To patriotic and charismatic leaders, it is here submitted, the problem of which indigenous language would, first, not be addressed in this way; and, second, not even arise in the case of Cameroon. These are very

---

⁹⁰ *Id.* at 36.
⁹¹ *Ibid.*
⁹² Cited in Fossungu, *supra*, note 2 at 100.
⁹³ Benjamin, *supra*, note 46 at 125: citing W.R. Johnson, *Africans-Speaking Africa? Lessons from the Cameroons* (autumn 1965) 1-2 *African Forum*).

controversial matters and one must share some of the misgivings some experts have raised about them (see below). But crisebacologists do not think we ought to avoid talking about issues (and just let sleeping dogs lie) simply because they are controversial. That would in fact be advocating against calling a spade a spade and hiding the traitors. As a notable democracy and good governance advocate, I fearlessly opened one of my discussions on the issues with, "A lot of people are afraid of controversy. But some of us just love it, because, as Funnyman once put it to me, *genuine intellectuals* do learn a lot from it."[94] I am thus inclined to think that the important thing has to do with one's ability to convincingly defend these theses. Therefore, let me very briefly school readers a little on *onesidetakism* (which opposes *giveantakism* or reciprocity in relationships[95]) before valiantly taking the manner of tackling the problems first and the creation of a problem out of a no-problem later.

As to the first point, Indonesia seems to stand out as a possible teacher. With one of the most sophisticated and cosmopolitan cultures of today's world, according to some North American researchers, Indonesia (Southeast Asia's largest country) is the world's fourth most populous country with some 200 million people of diverse ethnicity, sharing all the major religions of humankind and speaking some 80 distinct languages and about 240

---

[94] Peter Ateh-Afac Fossungu, "African Democracy vis-a-vis Western Democracy: Afrikenticating, Follyfying, Expibasketizing, and Reversing the 'African Democracy' Debate", in Munyaradzi Mawere and Tendai Rinos Mwanaka (eds.), *Democracy, Good Governance and Development in Africa* (Bamenda: Langaa RPCIG, 2015), 71-124 at 71 (original emphasis).

[95] See Fossungu, *supra*, note 85, chapters 1 & 2.

dialects.[96] Among other factors that have helped Indonesia to succeed where people in Cameroon (and Africa generally) will only be babbling and crying over nothing, are its charismatic and patriotic leaders who, "to solve the language problem confronting the world's largest archipelago, deliberately adopted an Indonesian minority language as a national language."[97] What is there really to prevent the UDA leadership from also sagaciously choosing one of such indigenous African languages, if there are vision and enthusiasm? *Enthusiastic* and *visionary* leadership must be capitalized since it is important to accentuate the fact that African freedom, unity and development are currently 'without Africa' and very ineffective most probably because the bulk of us, Africans, due to moneyintriguism and selfishness from (ir)rational choice, do not do what we are naturally good at. That frame of mind also necessarily motivates the putting of unqualified or incompetent people in positions of responsibility while keeping the right (able and enthusiastic) people out for ulterior considerations. This fact easily comes out in situations like the one in Cameroon, with ministers shying away from public functions because of the intensification of fears of cabinet reshuffle;[98] and those in the USA where the compromising of "both principles and prudence for the sake of party unity" led "prominent Republicans to present the country with a presidential nominee whom they themselves considered

---

[96] Satya Das, "Playing by the Rules in Indonesia: A Little Homework Goes a Long Way for Investors" *The Edmonton Journal* (26 December 1996), E1.

[97] *Ibid*.

[98] See Peter Ngea Beng, "Ministers Shy Away from Public Functions As Cabinet Reshuffle Fears Intensify" *The Herald* (Yaoundé, 1-2 December 1997), 1-2.

unfit for the office."⁹⁹ As I must emphasize, Africa cannot get into Africa with such a mindset because only competent and

---

⁹⁹ Ross Douthat, "The Dangers of Hillary Clinton" available @ http://www.nytimes.com/2016/10/23/opinion/sunday/the-dangers-of-hillary-clinton.html?ref=opinion&_r=. According to the *New York Times*, "Mr. Trump has no foreign policy experience. He has, however, received two briefings from American intelligence agencies that should have alerted him to the challenges facing the next president but apparently have not. All of which raises unsettling questions about whether the Republican nominee for the most powerful job in the world is Mr. Putin's poodle, stubbornly naïve, totally clueless or, as some have ominously suggested, protecting undisclosed business interests in Russia… What does matter is that with each new bizarre utterance he provides further proof of his inability to evaluate credible information and, more broadly, his lack of fitness to further his country's best interests." NYT Editorial Board, "Donald Trump's Weird World" @ http://www.nytimes.com/interactive/interactive/opinion/editorialboard.html/2016/10/12/.2016). Some commentators thus think "Trump is a marvellously efficient acid bath, stripping away his supporters' surfaces, exposing their skeletal essences." George F. Will, "Donald Trump is the GOP's Chemotherapy" @ https/www.washingtonpost.com/opinions/Donald-trumps-vile-candidacy-is-chemotherapy-for-the-gop/2016/10/10/73e40f30-8f05-11e6. Others hold that "the GOP's inability to stop Trump shows the party is unfit to lead the country." Robert Kagan, "Why We Shouldn't Forgive the Republicans Who Sold Their Souls" @ https/www.washingtonpost.com/opinions/the-cowardly-gop-has-engineered-its-own-suicide/2016/10/11/ec585af8-8f22-11e6a3-d500; with the Washington Post editors concluding that "his racist scheme dovetails with long-standing GOP tactics." Washington Post Editorial Board, "Donald Trump's Strategy for Minority Americans? Don't Let Them Vote" @ https://www.washingtonpost.com/opinions/trumps-strategy-for-minority-americans-don't-let-them-vote/2016/10/11/e3c509-8fe9-11e6.

enthusiastic African officials (like Dr Cho Ayaba of Ambazonia, Dr Arikana Chihombori-Quao of Zimbabwe and Prof. PLO Lumumba of Kenya) would be willing and able to fearlessly address questions such as the following HISOFE one that I once posed on the FIFA (*World* Football Federation, it is called?) sham:

> Has any of us ever seen a non-French (no matter how he or she might be more qualified than all the French on earth) coaching the French national team? And this does not apply to only the French, mark you. Look at Italy, England, Germany, the United States, and the rest. Why do we think FIFA would prohibit non-nationals (mostly our professionals there) from playing in national teams at World Cups, but say nothing about non-nationals (often their unemployed and/or retired professionals) coaching these same national teams? That is the piece of the puzzle I leave to Africans in particular to try to [grow up and] fit in.[100]

While the called-upon Africans are doing the figuring out, I will continue, on my part, with the hypocrisy issues that are laboriously standing in the way of Africa getting into Africa. For example, I have postulated elsewhere that the "hypocritical attitude that Immaculate Fossungu valiantly stood against in the coronation exercise is especially so glaring in the 'modern' African political sphere. This is precisely the reason anyone who (like Fon DF Fossungu and his upright daughter) does not take 'advantage' of

---

[100] Peter Ateh-Afac Fossungu, "When Will Cameroonians Ever Grow Up?" *The Herald* (Yaoundé, 20-21 July 1999), 19.

the lucrative crookedness is ridiculed. How glorious Africa has been reduced to this! Get Africa back into Africa!"[101] "Worse yet," declares another disappointed Africa-loving expert, "the resurgence of military coup d'état, the rancour, violence and apparent manipulations associated with elections, and the trend towards political settlement after electoral conflicts through the formation of coalition governments all indicate huge deficits of democracy in West Africa."[102]

Yet, these same political adventurers will go pouring champagne in the numerous economically-baseless palaces while the masses are going through untold suffering! Yes, you can easily see the same trends with these dictators (traitors, to be exact) in Africa endlessly using the folly of 'national unity' and 'secession' to keep the people in perpetual poverty and misery. Paul Biya of Cameroon and Mobutu of Zaire, do the experts hear you well? Certainly, and it is well known that "all these vices have never done anything good to Africa besides plunging the continent under a thick blanket of miasma and helplessness."[103] Partying to a fault

---

[101] Fossungu, *supra*, note 85 at 86.

[102] Richard Asante, "The State and Knowledge of Democracy in West Africa: A Critical Analysis", in Munyaradzi Mawere and Tendai Rinos Mwanaka (eds.), *Democracy, Good Governance and Development in Africa* (Bamenda: Langaa RPCIG, 2015), 157-92 at 158.

[103] Munyaradzi Mawere, Annastasia M. Mawere and Pedro Celso Jovo, "Culture, Ethics and Politics for a Better and Sustainable Africa: The Mozambican Experience", in Munyaradzi Mawere and Tendai Rinos Mwanaka (eds.), *Democracy, Good Governance and Development in Africa* (Bamenda: Langaa RPCIG, 2015), 269-95 at 269. See also Peter Ateh-Afac Fossungu, *The HISOFE Dictionary of Midnight Politics: Expibasketical Theories*

and competing only for the championship of the African Beer Drinking Cup of Nations (BDCN) in the Cameroon Goodwill Association of Montreal (CGAM) at yet another international level. Tie the entire scheme to the nonsensical urge to be seen externally as an Ideal spouse while being the Worst spouse internally.[104] Put all that comfortably in the same Hillary-*deplorable basket* of African dictators being hailed by the outside exploiters for whom they work to our internal detriment. No one seems to put this view better than Professor Asante of the University of Ghana does in stating that:

> Ake further argues that in Africa, the elite supported democracy only as a means to power, while international agencies supported it as an asset to structural adjustment and as a result, states in Africa got trapped between the demands of external donours for economic liberalization on the one hand, and the needs of political majorities on the other, leading to the creation of 'exclusionary democracies', which allow for political competition, but can't respond to majority demands in a meaningful way.[105]

African liberation, unity, and development *sans l'Afrique* indeed! Equate it with onesidetakism (another appropriate definition of the Africa-Europe relationship), if you will. "Onesidetakism opposes *giveantakism* (theory of give-and-take) which promotes collective

---

on *Afrikentication and African Unity* (Bamenda: Langaa RPCIG, 2015).
    [104] See Fossungu, *supra*, note 85, chapter 2.
    [105] Asante, *supra*, note 102 at 162.

progress, not the '*I, the only one*' mentality of onesidetakists and takebackists."[106] It is in this respect that crisebacologists do compellingly think that the Indonesian language-adoption methodology is praiseworthy despite the vain 'pleasing-the-West' criticisms against it. For example, there is the critique relating to the cost of achieving this one-national-language policy. "Economically", Bangbose has indicated as a critical line,

the choice of a minority language for wealth getting [and wealth sharing] is bound to result in under-employment and the emergence of an exploiting and wealthy minority politically and judicially, when law-making and justice are carried out in a language the majority does not and, in all likelihood, cannot control well, in the near future there are bound to be miscarriage of justice and the enrichment of political power in the hands of a few who manage to gain control of language. Socio-culturally, the only true way to develop our heritage is through the media of own language.[107]

Bangbose is certainly the kinds of people that Africa's so-called leaders must have surrounded themselves with; people who view things only in their own selfish interests. Call it onesidetakism, as you must. This is what is actually the problem in Africa; not the language-inflation in Africa as such. For a very banal example, wasn't there language-inflation in the 'New World' (North America) before the Founders of the USA chose English as the official language? According to President Nelson Mandela, "one of the problems we are facing in the world today are people who do not look at problems objectively, but from the point of view of their own interests. That makes things difficult because once a

---

[106] Fossungu, *supra*, note 85 at 64.
[107] Ajulo, *supra*, note 8 at 36.

person is not objective it is extremely difficult to reach an agreement."[108] I must reiterate that Mandela could not have been more correct, and I would like to use some other instances of useless African debates and a few further crisebacological questions to prop him up.

Debating without Understanding Debates and the African Virus of Biggytitlemania

Let me now take the CGAM discussion of issues pertaining to the membership of members' spouses in the January 2006 Goodwill General Assembly (GGA) to fasten up the irrationality functional demonstration of Africans' biggytitlemania (or love of empty-big titles or certificates) that is indisputably one famous Hercules standing in the way of African liberation and development. I have condemned it elsewhere as "Empty Literacy! Vapid Literacy! Upside-down Literacy! Isn't it time to level-headedly 'take-back' both the upside-down assistantship-education theory and thumb education thesis and other frustrations (including the biological) facing sweet-voicing African children?"[109] Said CGAM January Assembly, it must be pointed out, could not have put the final full-stop to the spousal debates. It only touched on their admission:

The May 2006 GGA took up the associated issues of their contributions and other financial matters. On membership of

---

[108] Cited in Fossungu, *supra*, note 94 at 99.
[109] Fossungu, *supra*, note 85 at 118.

members' spouses, the President [Paul Takha Ayah] informed the House of a suggestion that came up during a meeting of the Executive Bureau requesting that couples should pay $30.00 for entertainment so as to encourage members to enrol with their spouses. [Paul Takha Ayah would also be heard making the same logical argument in the January 2007 Assembly in response to Peter Fossungu's question regarding the equity of payment for the birth "social package"[110]].

The President further said that this issue was not covered by the bylaws but that it was necessary for the House to discuss it then. Vincent Cheg wanted to know the reason why some members' spouses do not want to join the association. The reasons are many and varied and also depend on the individuals concerned. Peter Fossungu and Ayuk Prudence were of the opinion that members are individuals and so the $20.00 contribution for entertainment should stand as such. This view was also supported by Fidelis Folifac. Berri Nsame's opinion was that those members' spouses who come on a regular basis and who are not registered members should be treated as regular visitors. Florence Nankam suggested that couples should pay $30.00 and singles $15.00. Denis Ako-Arrey insisted on singles continuing to pay $20 because 'that will encourage singles like us to get married.' Denis Alem was of the opinion that a $30.00 entertainment contribution by registered couples and $20.00 by singles would definitely help boost the morale of spouses to join. These opinions were put to vote and

---

[110] See Peter Ateh-Afac Fossungu, *Family Politics and Deception in Northern North America and West-Central Africa: Litigating God's Marriage Intention?* (Bamenda: Langaa RPCIG, 2015) chapter 4.

members voted overwhelmingly (18 to 9 votes) for registered couples paying $30.00 and all others $20.00 as entertainment contribution.[111]

Figure #1: Three CGAM Presidents: Paul Takha Ayah (2nd), Fidelis Folefac (4th), & Peter A. Fossungu (1st) Source: Cameroon Goodwill Association of Montreal

---

[111] Goodwill General Assembly (GGA) Minutes, May 2006.

Readers can obviously see here, first, that CGAMers (like Africans generally) seem to be interested only in numbers, not the quality that the Immaculate Freedom, Unity and Development (IFUD) Theory would require. Just look at the vast number of so-called *independent* states on the African continent (54 countries and still counting[112]) and their number on the North American (just 3 countries) to better grasp the thesis. To some experts, this straightforward observation may properly be raising the structure/agency debate which amounts to *structuralism* privileging structure and downplaying the role of agents, while *intentionalism* privileges the role of agents and downplays the role of structure – with both sets of debaters treating the meta-theoretical issues as a *dualism*, that is, as an either/or issue.[113] Professor David Marsh of the Australian National University and several others do not think the issues ought to be viewed in this way, preferring them to be considered as a *duality*. This means that we should see the relationship between the two elements of each pair as *interactive* and *iterative*, making the argument to instead run in this way: 1) *Structures* provide the context within which *agents* act but agents interpret structures and in acting change them, with these 'new' structures becoming the context within which agents act; and 2) *Material relations* provide the contexts within which *ideas* develop and

---

[112] In addition to Ambazonia, the following candidates are at the gate already knocking or contemplating knocking: Biafra (Nigeria), Kantanga (DRCongo), Tigray (Ethiopia), Ududuwa (Nigeria)……

[113] David Marsh, "Meta-Theoretical Issues", in David Marsh and Gerry Stoker (eds.), *Theory and Methods in Political Science* 3rd edition (London: Palgrave Macmillan, 2010), 212-31 at 212-13.

operate, but ideas are what are used to interpret those material relations and these interpretations help to change the material relations. These 'new' material relations become the context within which ideas develop.[114]

Secondly, CGAMers (like Africans generally) are thus solely interested in having couples join as couples without also considering the fairness of this to single persons, just like Bangbose et al do not bother about the minority (see below). Similarly, those who created the AU are just interested in having all the mini-states of the continent caged in there without any effect on both continental and global politics.[115] Otherwise, why is the AU funded by the same exploiters of Africa, and not by Africans themselves? Can you really be independent of your banker? Thirdly, CGAMers are also 'intentionally' ignoring the fact that the CGAM is an individual-membership association and not a couple-membership one – not to belabour the issue of commitment and dedication to the goals of the group. Not too surprising therefore that the CGAM died totally in 2018, just as the AU should have, but is still there for no other reason than to perpetually stifle the

---

[114] *Id* at 213.

[115] As a 'four-eyes' observer, I have similarly argued in *The HISOFE Dictionary of Midnight Politics* that "The question that may be asked concerns whether these calls were just after quantity or were they also considering quality and progress? Also, one can be very suspicious of the hidden agenda behind such calls, as several portions of this book would confirm, giving you the somewhat strategic reasons for this move. But more importantly, do people ever value anything they just 'pick up with their left hand' as the saying goes? In my experience, I have never seen any association that loosens all restrictions to its membership and succeeds." Fossungu, *supta*, note 103 at 157.

need for Africans genuinely uniting against the common adversaries – colonialism and perpetual enslavement under phony covers of independence and sovereignty. For a practical CGAM illustration that necessarily falls out from my detailed analysis of 'Death *Sociopackism* Compensation Rules and Visionlessness',[116] if Mrs X and Miss Y both lose their fathers, the CGAM pays each the $1500.00 sociopackism. The next day it is Mr X's dad and the CGAM pays $1500.00 to him without considering that the Xs are a couple. This CGAM encouragement of scholaparentistic financial calculations is similar, for instance, to the incessant highlighting of the corruption of African Presidents (by Western sources especially) without mentioning that of the multinational corporations and other foreigners corrupting these presidents; and is not the only issue though. You have just seen how the discussion and vote for the $30 spousal package was to encourage both of them to be CGAMers. But just hear what followed in the same doctors-charged Assembly:

> The next issue put to a vote was that a member who comes with an unregistered spouse (regular visitor) be allowed to pay the same $30.00 fee as registered couples or the visiting wife [or husband] should pay $20.00 as any other regular visitor. A yes vote was for visiting (regular) spouses to pay $20.00 as any other visitor. The Secretary General was of the opinion that it will also encourage the visiting spouses to become members as soon as possible if the same $30

---

[116] See Fossungu, *supra*, note 110 at 93-117.

entertainment contribution is applied to the couples too.[117]

Was all this not just a waste of time and energy by conspicuously certificateful-headed people who just don't know exactly what they are arguing about and why? Ambassador Dr Arikana Chihombori-Quao calls it noise-making on the leaves and branches, but doing absolutely nothing about the root of the tree that is responsible for its existence. You will not encounter anything different in Johannesburg in that misnamed structure called African Parliament! Just big certificates coming from the colonial education's 'service disciplines', isn't it? Yes, of course, Gospel according to Professor Ephraim Taurai Gwaravanda of Great Zimbabwe University who has firmly theorised that "the Eurocentric capitalist hegemony creates 'service disciplines' that justify capitalist rationality and meet capitalistic objectives rather than the poverty condition of Africans."[118] His theory goes very deeply into the heart of Africa's underdevelopment. What we need is African education for Africa! That is the correct path to African liberation and development, a route that would surely exclude wanton extortion from African administrators and those foreigners forcing these dictators on Africans.

---

[117] GGA Minutes, *supra*, note 111.

[118] Ephraim Taurai Gwaravanda, "The Impoverished African and the Poverty of Colonially Inherited Education in Africa", in Munyaradzi Mawere (ed.), *The Political Economy of Poverty, Vulnerability and Disaster Risk Management: Building Bridges of Resilience, Entrepreneurship and Development in Africa's 21st Century* (Bamenda: Langaa RPCIG, 2018), 255-77 at 255.

That brings us full circle to the few pertinent questions that may need to be answered by the types of unpatriotic onesidetakist advocates like Bangbose. Let's just take Bangbose's last sentence of his critique of the Indonesian Formula, for instance, and ask him and colleagues what becomes of the minority's own 'heritage development' when *only* the majority's language *must* be the media? In other words, to employ my apt viewpoint on the understanding of confusion, "It is not clear (absent confusion) why anyone should be talking of the respect of minority rights in the first place when the 'majority' *must always* prevail."[119] Next, let them also tell us clearly how the English (and/or French, Portuguese, Spanish) language(s) ever was/were the African majority's language(s) when the invading Europeans made it/them the 'media' of our 'only true way to develop our heritage'? It is now very obvious that the dependency syndrome would never permit Africans make even half a step forward, but rather hundreds steps backward continually. The much heralded CGAM administration of Dr Fidelis Folefac is also guilty of the dependency 'offence' in its own unique way. The much-sung visibility that the CGAM acquired during Folefac's terms of office (2008-2009) actually cost the association a lot in its auto-development or self-help foundation. In other words, that administration completely reverted the CGAM to the trend currently in Africa of relying wholly on others (the LaSalle Borough and Police, for instance) for things that the group was supposed to work hard in permanently acquiring. I am talking of such things as foreseen in the "2006 President's Vision" and the impressive

---

[119] Fossungu, *supra*, note 2 at 67 (original emphasis).

Goodwill Projects Committee (GPC) Report of the same year.[120] The questionable trend could basically be approximated to nonoselfism or visionlessness and to the absence of Scholasticalization (or the enthusiasm to succeed[121]) and would thus perfectly validate the experts' argument "that Western education imposed by the colonizers creates a dependency syndrome whereby the colonized always rely on the colonial master for ideas and epistemological constructs."[122] Most of these things occurred in the CGAM mostly through the Folefacist vexatious scrapping of the birth and marriage sociopackism and the unorthodox use of adhocism or motioncracy.[123] In short, the CGAM at this time was riding high in external profile but not benefitting CGAMers at all. The association seems to have been used to further selfish agendas, intimately explaining perhaps why it is President Folefac (and not the CGAM) that got the 2010 honour from the LaSalle Borough.[124]

Thirdly, we need to find out from the Bangbose-like critics whether our 'heritage' is truly developed now that things are still

---

[120] As to more of both of which, see Peter Ateh-Afac Fossungu, *Historical and Partyological Postponement of Democracy in Canada: Elongating the Business Pleasure War in Africa?* (Saarbrucken, Germany: LAP Lambert Academic Publishers, 2018) at 120-27.

[121] See Fossungu, *supra*, note 85, chapter 4.

[122] Gwaravanda, *supra*, note 118 at 255.

[123] See Fossungu, *supra*, note 110, chapter 4.

[124] See LaSalle, "2010 Moulins d'Or Community Award: Fidelis Folifac" @ www.http.ville.montreal.qu.ca/pls/portal/docs/page/arrond_1st_en/media/document/folefac.

being done 'through the means of our own language' (I should just guess that Bangbose must be a European who has just adopted an African-sounding name?). And, fourthly, whether it is the adoption of a minority African language in most of the African countries that has today actually resulted in the blatant existing 'enrichment of political power in the hands of a few' as well as furthering unsatisfactory employment in Africa? In short, I just need to close the matter by clarifying that patriotic leaders/people do not reason in this way, instead putting the interests of the country and progeny above their personal aggrandizement. The Indonesian leaders were sharp enough (which might usually be possible only in the midst of patriotism and objectivity) to realize that "they could not build a nation by imposing the majority language on dozens of minorities. Today, Bahasa Indonesia is well established and spoken as a second language by most Indonesians."[125]

In Cameroon, on the other hand, there has only been a monumental failure on the part of the Ahidjo-Biya regime to even satisfy people like Bangbose by 'imposing' (through their *pleins pouvoirs*) such a single indigenous national language (majority or minority). As enlightenment and democracy are said to actually be two sides of the same coin, free-thinking and self-ruled African leaders cannot even want to impose, or even appear as forcing, their own language in such a scenario. Indonesia seems to have clearly said so a few minutes ago and in spite of the critiques that may be levelled against their policy, it is wiser and more pragmatic that those in power do everything to avoid unduly enhancing their privileged position by imposing their language on the powerless. That is often the spark to secessionist drives: exactly what is now

---

[125] Cited in Fossungu, *supra*, note 2 at 165.

happening in Cameroon with the brainless high-handed imposition of the French language and civil law on Anglophone schools and lawyers. The UDA can simply not afford to go down this road. The debate on this language point is surely to continue as the critics have amply indicated, but Cameroon has been truly blessed but cursed.

Patriotically Embracing the God-given Blessings: The Nobisooh Health Centre Speech – What Happened to the Liberating 99-Sensism?

What is more significantly graphical to the point here is the fact that progressive, far-sighted, and devoted Cameroonian leaders would have quickly discovered that this vexed problem of indigenous language choice in Cameroon was a superfluous one. I would think the problem (of which indigenous language to adopt) would not even come up to such Cameroon-loving leaders because there is actually in Cameroon a non-indigenous non-foreign language that most Cameroonians, English-speaking and French-speaking, do understand and speak.[126] Let me leave the academic wrangling concerning the utility of the Pidgin language and solidify its generality in use with the Health Centre palaver, coming from what Ambazonians now call Lebialemzone (what LRC calls Lebialem Division). While doing the buttressing job, the Alou administrator's speech also raises a lot of other pertinent issues. If there is any doubt about the overturning of Africa through colonial

---

[126] See Fossungu, *supra*, note 2 at 161-66; and Ngefac, *supra*, note 43.

education and languages, then just listen now to the deeds of the Alou District Officer (D.O.) that would not only just openly expose the 99-sensers' minus-one essential sense but just also vouch well for the stark absence of pre-colonial good governance characteristics like accountability, transparency, and the like in *modern* African administrators. Where to with them, Africa, except to underdevelopment and perpetual poverty for the masses?

I must just let you listen crisebacologically to the D.O. as he wantonly interrupted the traditional enthronement rites of South Africa-based Chief Formbuehndia Bernard Mbancho on 19 October 2002 in Nwangong and threateningly passed his financial responsibilities to the Nwangong people (with his signature 'No bi sooh?') amidst the 'Chief Foletia-instigated' clapping. Call it 'Royal Upsidedowning of Africa', if you like, and crisebacological Nwangongers would not object to that at all. Hear the *nchinda* administrator interminably *districtofficializing* in Pidgin:

> My brothers and sisters, notables, elites, His Royal Highness, and sons and daughters (because some of you are my children)! I would want to turn and talk in the popular language which is Pidgin so that each and everyone here can understand this message well.
>
> We all know that during cry-die a lot of other things are done and settled. We, Banyangi (of course, you all know that I am from Banyangi land), often say that many things, including even quarrels, are resolved in a 'die-house': *No bi sooh?* [Of course, the grieving population agreed with him with a sonorous '*Na so*' and he, therefore, proudly carried

on, undaunted by the feared 99-Sensism[127]. I am here with my collaborators.... [who he took all the time and formality to introduce, one by one, amidst clapping for each of them]. We are here to join you in mourning one of ours, our lost brother, and I want to see that important tradition of yours

---

[127] 99-Sensesim is a theory or concept that is better grasped with knowledge of Cameroon Ethnic Epithetization Politics (CEEP) – a formidable anti-liberation tool meant for 'divide, conquer and enslave'. *Ethnic Epithetization* is consequently just as popular in Cameroon as is soccer, a sport which competes for supremacy only with beer-drinking and the hopelessly unthinking nature thereto associated. National liberation movements must, therefore, beware of this cankerworm! As Fossungu (*supra*, note 2 at 200 n.200) has philosophically observaquestioned, "the 'hungry man, angry man' adage would seem to have no place in this country. What about the 'drunkard, unthinking man' adage?" I am not here to engage in responding to the question but simply to give readers some few examples of the CEEP from an African dictionary on 'the Tensions of Belonging in Cameroon'. According to that dictionary, *Famla* or a sort of witch-crafting way of making wealth is pinned on the hard-working Bamileke of Bamboutouszone. This is what is often described by some experts as *nyongo* – a money-giving, human-eating cult. The label for the Béti of Sanagazone is *Chop Broke Potism* or people who do not think of tomorrow with money. For females of the Banyangi ethnic group of Debundschazone, it is *Ashawo* or prostitutes; and for people from Savannazone generally, it is *Came-No-Go*. Like most of these ethnic groups in Cameroon, the epithet of Debundschazone's Bangwa is 99-Sense. The explanatory attachment being that these Bangwa are so craftily clever that they would not sell you a hen (but only a cock) for fear that the hen would produce chicken for you, and thus prevent your coming back to buy from them. See Peter Ateh-Afac Fossungu, *Africa's Anthropological Dictionary on Love and Understanding: Marriage and the Tensions of Belonging in Cameroon* (Bamenda: Langaa RPCIG, 2014) at xi.

before I and my delegation can go away because we also have another event to attend to in another part of the sub-division, precisely in Ndungatet. Do you think I can be able to witness it? [Of course, again, the answer was obvious: 'Yes, of course!'] Okay, you should better make it short so that we too can get the essentials before taking our leave [but he himself was not leaving the people to continue with the enthronement rites].

What I would like, however, to take a bit of your time to harp on is in relation to the Health Centre. There have been several reports to me that the woman in whose house the Health Centre was operating has driven the workers from there. All this is because she wants to be compensated with some small amount of money. It got to the point where she even *'threw contree melecine'* in the premises. That is why I had sent a message to the Fon to see to it that the Health Centre is removed from there: since no one would be comfortable going to a cursed building like that to receive the medicines and other healthcare services that are needed. It is useless to have a Health Centre stocked with medicines whereas people cannot go *'helep demself for dey: no bi sooh?'*

So, I had beseeched the Fon to move the Health Centre and he has already informed me that this has been done. I am, therefore, thanking the Fon for such efficient action. But the good work is not yet over because we have to have a permanent place where to house the Health Centre. That means that the Fon has to allocate the land for that, and I am advising all of you to abide by the Fon's decision. Thus, if the Fon will point to any spot as the place, then you should sacrifice by ceding that land for the Health Centre. The chosen piece of land must also have to be in an area where the population is dense. My suggestion is that, from November (next month), I will be here for the Fon to show me the chosen land. I am calling on you all, brothers and sisters, to aid us with the money for cement and other materials for the building of the Health Centre. We will also need people like construction technicians to volunteer their services; no one must have to be paid for helping to erect the Health Centre. The only thing anyone can ask for will be food: provided there would even be a little bit of money available for that. The issue of payment is completely out of the question because this Health Centre is for all of us.

And let me assure you that you should not think that your financial contributions would be diverted to personal use by the D.O. or the Fon: since it is almost ten months now without me hearing of any palaver from Nwangong. This demonstrates clearly that you're very lucky to have a wonderful Fon. *No bi sooh?* [Clapping].

Would you then be afraid to send money to me through the Fon? No. Hence, a committee would be formed for the purpose, with the Fon heading it. I would only be in it to watch over the money like a dog to make sure no one 'touches' the money; in which case I will pounce on that person. I myself would not touch it, and I wouldn't even want to touch it. I want to make sure whatever you have sent is used just for the purpose you sent the money. Let me not take so much of your time by talking a lot, being happy that the president of your Cultural and Development

Association (NWACUDA) [that is Paul Agafina] is even right here beside me.

I would like all the elites here present to spread this news to other Nwangong people when they get back to their various bases. When money is sent, the committee would be reporting to the D.O. about any amount so sent. The D.O. would then decide what to be buying until the job is completely done. As indicated earlier, I wouldn't want to take much of your time since I myself am very keen on witnessing the *contree fashion* in relation to the new Chief that just came in. Would I be able to witness that *contree fashion* before leaving, please? [Agreement signalled] So then, you people should hurry over it so that I can be a part of it before going to the other event in Ndungatet. Thank you all very much; His Royal Highness, thank you.[128]

---

[128] Alou District Officer, private communication, 19 October 2002.

Figure #2: The Alou Administration (D.O. with walking stick, Mayor on his left) when they just arrived at the Chief Formbuehndia funeral on 19 October 2002

Source: Benji Photo-Video, Dschang

There was, certainly, what Cameroonians are very good at, of course. Clapping without questioning, that is. This speech has been worth reading and discussing, not just because of what was said but especially also to expose the mysteriousness in knowing exactly what these 'modern' African government officials actually do with the state budget that is put at their disposal, that it is instead the local population that must then carry out projects for the government that these centrally-appointed officials are there representing. The mystery drastically augments with the fact that Chief Foletia Vincent (who is supposed to better know and defend the tradition and culture) had then taken over the microphone (after the D.O.) and proudly recapped the D.O.'s long-lasting talk in Bangwa: since some of the villagers don't quite grasp even the Pidgin the D.O. was using. The Nwangong Chief did not just 'translate' but actually was telling the people of Nwangong to quickly wake up from sleep and make sure they build the Health Centre as demanded by the D.O.: knowing that the D.O. would thereafter obviously 'help' them with a "hefty envelope" toward the project. So many questions are raised and I trust the intelligence of readers enough not to bother attempting to think that I can raise all of these queries for them.

Are Nwangong elites (meaning *school-gone*) just 'elites' only in the business of sucking the poor villagers dry in like manner of their counterparts at the national and provincial levels? I am here referring to the French government coming to these people's aid and some of the locals, again, turning it to an occasion to hoodwink the local population with a so-called apportioned contribution as 'their' own share – all thanks to the non-existence of notions of accountability and transparency in their thinking. Just listen to Peter Ngunyi Asahchop's letter to Momany, to grasp what I have been struggling to say:

> I was in the village a few days ago and Mamie Regina was from Kounghow to consult but nothing very serious because she travelled there herself. However, as an aged person, she complains always of not being sound, and that

is normal with aged people. The village is undertaking a water project sponsored by the French government in the entire Lebialem Division and our village happens to be one of the villages chosen. The village has to contribute 500,000 francs as their own share. The water project starts from Kounghow in Fonjumetaw down to the Palace and all people who have houses and plots at Letia are taxed more than people from other quarters. Please, your contribution is very necessary as both an elite and as a man with a plot around Letia; that is both men and women.[129]

What French government that has unilaterally decided to help them would then be demanding money from the villagers in order to do so? Moneyintriguism is obviously a huge obstacle to African liberation and progress, being easily perceived in the constant hijacking of the agendas of national liberation movements by externally funded bodies such as Non-Governmental Organizations (NGOs). The most crucial thing right now is that the Alou administrative officer's speech was delivered in the God-furnished common national language. But rather than formally elevate it to its rightful place (like Ambazonians are already proudly doing), this language will instead be denigrated; a language which is popularly downgraded as Pidgin English. According to some informed Canadian sources, this Pidgin "grew up in the Orient [in imperialist days], and it has often been suggested that one motive for, perhaps wholly unconscious and perhaps not, developing pidgin English

---

[129] Peter Ngunyi Asahchop, private communication, 3 June 1999, paragraph 4.

was to make non-English speakers sound foolish and ignorant."[130] Whatever the motive for its development may be, the Pidgin in Cameroon is very unlike the 'Broken English' that will be found in other former English colonies in Africa. Cameroon's unique lingua franca has been largely brought about by the numerous European influences Africa has known. It is unique to Cameroon and I actually realized this when I arrived in neighbouring Nigeria in the early 1980s. The Pidgin-speakers there could hardly grasp my own Cameroon Pidgin, whereas I could almost perfectly understand their own 'Broken English' simply because of my also understanding 'good' English. Cameroon's version is unique probably because of the multiple foreign influences the country, unlike most other African states, has been exposed to. Several experts have shown how and why this unique version of Pidgin is a common uniting language to Cameroonians.[131] What then could properly account for the gapping failure of Cameroon's administrators in this made-easy field of common national language? The probable convincing answer is intimately tied to the issue of whether there can even be effective bilingualism in this country in view of the secret accords with France, agreements that are the hot subject matter of Dr Arikana Chihombori-Quao's valiant stand-off with France and its African puppets like Moussa Faki of Chad, the current AU Commission Chairperson! What do you then realistically expect from that body in relation to African freedom and progress?

---

[130] Frye, *supra*, note 14 at 23.
[131] See Fossungu, *supra*, note 2 at 162-65 and the numerous sources therein discussed, including Ngefac, *supra*, note 43.

CHAPTER 3
CAN THERE BE EFFECTIVE BILINGUALISM IN CAMEROON WITH THE SECRET AGREEMENTS WITH FRANCE?

The question of the genuineness of official bilingualism in Cameroon remains one of the most vexing of topical issues, beautifully epitomized by the current quagmire in the two English-speaking regions – Debundschazone and Savannazone (aka Ambazonia). These are authentic names, respectively, for what many people continue to dully call Southwest and Northwest. To that misnaming, crisebacologists just say NO! They are justly Debundschazone (DBZ) and Savannazone (SVZ). The other eight regions (as just well-argued out by the Afrikenticators) truthfully are just: Adamawazone (ADZ), Bamboutouszone (BBZ), Benouezone (BNZ), Guinean-Savannazone (GSZ), Logonezone (LGZ), Nyongzone (NYZ), Sanagazone (SNZ), and Wourizone (WRZ).[132] Do just, therefore, abandon all the colonial directional names, please. These suggested names of Cameroon's administrative regions and their unofficial abbreviations constitute a small step in the mind-set decolonization process, no doubt! That is just, however, not just what we just should be just debating on just right now. The gapping failure in adopting a common national language in Cameroon can only be properly understood from the manner through which Cameroon's so-called leaders even got to possess the (in this instance unused) *pleins pouvoirs*, capped by the 'secret agreements with France' on a range of fields – all aimed at maintaining French colonialism and propagating the French

---
[132] See Fossungu, *supra*, note 2 at 4.

language and culture.[133] Because of these illicit accords, some curse has apparently been taking over blessings due to the uncultured turning of deaf ears to sane counsel that:

> Assimilation promotes only regression in human rights and that is surely not what Africa deserves from its leader (Cameroon). Africa is not especially interested in having a leader who, moreover, does not genuinely seek to know what holds a society together, where the society is going, nor how it is getting there. Until all these vital issues are properly addressed in Africa, there is just no point in employing terms like democracy and biculturalism in this continent, a continent that would then… simply continue to remain 'a blank area of natural resources to be exploited by countries that are more advanced and better organized than we [Africans] are because they've spent more on their education.'[134]

Cursing Cameroon's Multifaceted Blessings for Leading Africa?

Let me answer by first putting a little *accent* on the appealing music from Cameroon before continuing with other cultural aspects such as dancing from Bangwaland. Cameroon is actually more than

---

[133] See Bjornson, *supra*, note 70 at 114-15; & Victor T. Le Vine, "Political-Cultural Schizophrenia in Francophone Africa", in I.J. Mowoe and Richard Bjornson (eds.), *Africa and the West: The Legacies of Empires* (New York: Greenwood Press, 1986), 159-73 at 163-69.

[134] Fossungu, *supra*, note 2 at 244 (omission is added).

blessed in numerous domains to lead Africa out of the dungeon. Cameroon music has something that charms. Let the Douala come in here to cement the point for Africans and the rest of the world. Makossa comes from the Douala in Wourizone but had already become something of a national (and continental) music before the French *nchinda* called President Paul Biya came up and 'pleins-pouvoirsly' decided that Cameroon must become his ethnic group, his New Ethnic Group.[135] That is, by his using 'national' TV and Radio to promote only Beti music called Bikutsi (which is equally electrifying but more 'porn-like' and noisier). Ange Bagnia and others like Grace Decca have already sufficiently told Mr. President and the likes of him that Makossa can never be killed. "*Que ceux qui dissent que le Makossa est mort lèvent leurs mains!*"[136] That is Ange Bagnia (a Bamileke from Bamboutouszone for that matter) singing in one of her touching tunes in which she proudly invites us to "dance it [Makossa] with the elegance that is of its very nature" like you can see Momany doing in Figure #3.

---

[135] Biya, *supra*, note 25 at 30.

[136] I wonder though if all this is still true internationally, with all the fuss that is now on social media ardently calling for the banning of world-dominating Nigerian music in Cameroon.

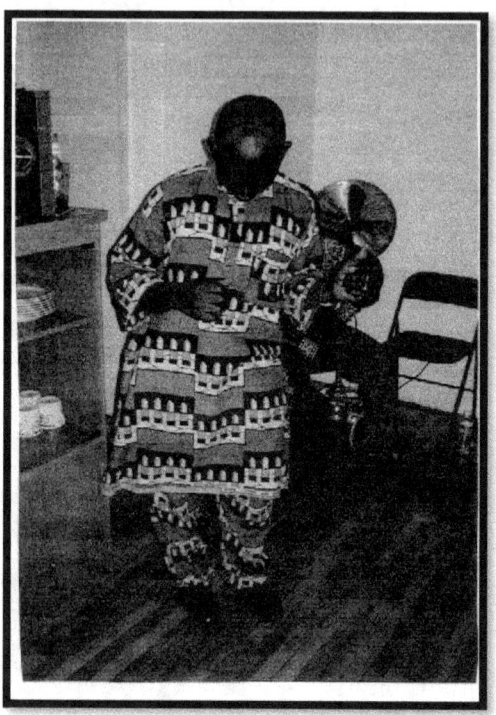

Figure #3: Momany just doing his thing: Dancing with elegance
Source: Momany Fossungu

To continue deeply critiquing Monsieur Paul Biya's ridiculous idea of seeking and promoting one-culture multiculturalism, here is the essential musical-biggytitlemania point. Dr Joseph O. Mankoe is from Ghana and was one of my three apartment mates at the University of Alberta. Unfortunately, when I left them and returned to Cameroon in 1992, I failed to maintain contact for quite some time with a lot of them in Edmonton, including Rev. Dalton and Ruby Grant (the Black American family that even accompanied me to the airport)! It is quite a lengthy tale of heart-breaking encounters on my return that have no legitimate space here; some eye-opening biggytitlemania bits of which can nevertheless be picked up from Dr Mankoe's 6th and 8th paragraphs:

> I was sorry to learn of the break in your marriage [plans]. I had the sense that she was a woman you loved and cherished, and if absence makes the heart grow fonder, I would expect that your marriage would even be cemented with your two years of departure from her. Well, since you are now happily married, and there is no use crying over spilt milk, let sleeping dogs lie… Did you say you are doing a master's programme at McGill? I thought this time you would embark upon a PhD programme since, according to you, the university jobs at home were asking for a PhD.[137]

---

[137] Joseph O. Mankoe, private communication, 31 March 1996.

Figure #4: Momany on Graduation Day in November 1992 posing with Dr Joseph Mankoe above & with the Grants (Ruby & Dalton) below
Source: Momany Fossungu's Album

Oh Afrika! This biggytitlemania again and again! It makes me to always reflect on Nancy Whistance-Smith's eye-opening counsel in 2000 that 'God never had a Ph.D.' Yet he is the one who created the world, including those having the PhDs plus! But, most importantly, just hear what Dr Mankoe says in relation to one of Cameroon's cursed blessings in the third paragraph of his aforementioned 9-paragraph letter:

> I should now say that, although belated as you rightly acknowledged, your letter has cleared a lot of misgivings. Yes, and the Makossa music would simply not permit me to erase your memory out of my mind. The rich instrumental rhythms interspersed with golden male voices and harmonised with soothing female voices were and are capable of raising a man's low spirits. That is why although I don't understand the language I love the music, to say the least. I still play them, never get bored. It would have been nice to hear new ones. Your very name 'Fossungu' sounded musical in my ears. You remember when I tried to have fun with the name like: Fogunsu, Fussongo, Gussonfu? It was all because I liked the name.[138]

Dr Mankoe of Ghana is not alone though, and not only Africans would add to the long list because my non-African colleagues equally just can't get enough of Cameroon's Makossa and dishes; food types that trying to catalogue is a futile exercise that would even prevent us from doing the dancing we are now on. But permit some small space for this fastening food case before we continue

---

[138] *Ibid.*

with the dancing, since good dancing can hardly be exhibited on an empty stomach. Ferdinand Nkwetta of the Buea University School of Journalism would have told readers better what the assorted food-types point being made essentially is when he voiced it out in Nwangong Fondom in July 2014, just like Professor Emmanuel Anyefru has penned it in 2011.[139] But, not to stay with it in Cameroon entirely, take a 2002 'Appreciation Card' to Scholastica Achankeng Asahchop, whose "cooking compares to none."[140] The card was signed by a lot of the persons that Scholastica interacted with during her training at the Concordia University Women's Centre in Montreal (Canada), with Bita Eslami signing in with: "Scholastica, your input and sharing of experience were priceless & thanks for always letting me have bites of great cooking. All the best. Love. Bita Eslami." *Sans commentaire*! Flint, on her part, simply said "Scholastica, you rock!" This talk of someone rocking smoothly takes us back to the suspended dancing.

If you can rock or dance well to Cameroon's assorted types of music (Amumba, Bendskin, Bikutsi, Bottle Dance, Chamassi, Clokke, Makassi, Makossa, Njang, Ntegh, etc.), there is no dance in the world that would baffle you. Let's then doff our hats and thank Elvis Kemayou (from hard-working Bamileke land in Bamboutouszone) for his brilliance in creating and instituting *Dance Cameroon Dance*. This is a superb national-unity TV programme (comparable to America's *So You Think You Can Dance*) which was

---

[139] See Emmanuel Anyefru, 'The Refusal to Belong: Limits of the Discourse on Anglophone Nationalism in Cameroon" 28(2) *The Journal of Third World Studies* (2011), 277-306.

[140] Peter Ateh-Afac Fossungu, *Africans in Canada: Blending Canadian and African Lifestyles*? (Bamenda: Langaa RPCIG, 2013) at 122.

soon killed by seizing the very popular programme from Elvis and handing it to Monsieur Biya's incompetent and lazy *chop-broke-pottist* tribesman. What else has this 'French nchinda' (who has never been seen in African attire like the ones in Figures #3 & #1 above) not done to crucify rich African culture? It is certainly the handiwork of rootless certificateful empty-head *intellectuals*. Italicized because these are intellectuals who only know (from their upsidedownised colonial education) how to endlessly victimize the very people they are supposed to be liberating, leading and protecting! Sickening indeed! It has never been any part of authentic African culture for its intellectuals to be predators to the very people and culture that these intellectuals should be guarding and protecting. As a female Bangwa Chief who is based in Maryland (USA) has ably theorized, "Leaders do not destroy. They protect, they repair, they guide, they caution and they communicate effectively."[141] What obtains today in this continent is deliberate and calculated upsidedownism, better described by some as "African Overseas Culture". There is just nothing like accountability or transparency with these colonially schooled people in positions of authority.

For illustration, take the case of the government of Cameroun brazenly profiting from the tragedy of its population rather than aiding them out of it with the massive foreign assistance received. Readers would thus hear Dr Boniface Forbin editorialising in 1998 about an oil tanker accident and spill in Nsam (Cameroon) that:
Going beyond restoring the survivors' health, didn't the public understand that with so much foreign aid that came in, something would be done to rehabilitate the survivors within a wider

---

[141] Cited in Fossungu, *supra*, note 85 at 20 n.1.

programme of poverty alleviation in Nsam? We think that families that survived the disaster should have benefited from social infrastructure like portable water, a good medical clinic, better drainage, and even relocation of families whose houses were close to the SCDP tanks.[142]

How can this type of corrupt and corrupting *intellectuals* ever think of, let alone effect, African liberation? I do not really need to displace other people's versions and be the one to tell readers a lot about the corruption-degree of Cameroon's state counsels, lawyers and magistrates, gendarmes and other administrators, and what have you. If you really think I should and the detailed account of Fossungu[143] is too far off, then Boniface Forbin's remarks in relation to the Nsam Disaster would be appropriate here as well because all this nonsense cannot be happening without the knowledge of those higher up. As *The Herald* editor has then put it:

> Madeline Fouda, minister of social welfare, has not been kind to the Nsam disaster victims. She accuses them of asking too much from the government. But she fails to state what the government has done to help with the poverty situation of Nsam village. Can't the government also have the honour to make a statement on how much relief aid has been received and how it intends to use it? We note also in this regard that so far the report of inquiry ordered by the government on the Nsam disaster remains

---

[142] Boniface Forbin, "Herald Editorial – Nsam Disaster: Government is still Owing" *The Herald* (Yaoundé, 3-4 August 1998), 4.

[143] *Supra*, note, chapter 2.

unpublished, months after the 45-day deadline. We think the government ought to show a lot more understanding for the survivors even if it refuses to be open on the issue.[144]

Educated administrators indeed! And very patriotic ones at that! Moreover, these are the same *elites* who are ignorantly using the useless talk of witchcraft in the villages to frighten Africans off their authentic roots! Just staying true to the secret pacts, of course? With such secret (and, therefore, illicit) agreements then, it is not clear how anyone who is party to them can ever be genuinely talking of pride in diversity (linguistic and others) in Cameroon. This is so, whether one considers the pre-1996 or post-1996 periods.

Pre-1996 Bilingualism: The Authenticity of English and Ngoalingualism

In Cameroon, therefore, not only is the adoption of a common national indigenous Cameroonian language inhibited by the 'secret agreements' with France on the terms of which these national traitors are maintained in power. In addition, even the making of both foreign colonially inherited languages (English and French) effective official languages is similarly put out. This is no idle talking on my (or anyone else's) part. Several reports have attested to the fact that it is just empty preaching of bilingualism. I have provided a lengthy catalogue of some of them.[145] The so-called

---

[144] Forbin, *supra*, note 142.
[145] See Fossungu, *supra*, note 2 at 168-75.

Université de Yaoundé (the brainchild of Ngoa-lingualism[146]) is a fitting example in the fields of the 'secret agreements' and has itself followed almost the same name-change path as the country itself. I have also very elaborately discussed some intriguing 'Theories Drawn From the Country's Name-Changing Justifications'.[147] As to the Université de Yaoundé (UNIYAO), for instance, it is often claimed that the institution and its programmes are bijural and bilingual. But it must be noted that bijuralism and bilingualism are expected only of the Anglophone students, leading to Professor Jacques Benjamin's euphemism of being *'bilingue en français'*.[148] Quite apart from more recent researches from Etchu and Grundstorm[149] and Harry Kuchah Kuchah,[150] another university

---

[146] "What is Ngoa-lingualism? Perhaps only the experiences of some newly arrived to the Ngoa [Yaoundé University] campus could better explain it to you. They would tell you Ngoa-lingualism means unilingualism under the camouflage of bilingualism. It should thus not be surprising to find that one of the newly arrived Anglophone male students to the unique Yaounde University would, for instance, go to the University's restaurant (*Resto*) and, on being handed a plate (*plateau*) of food without the usual pineapple (*anana*), would stare on, not knowing what to say, since he must speak French to be understood in his bilingual Cameroon. When those lined up behind him would shout out: *Allez-y, Anglo!* (anything that doesn't go well is Anglophone in this institution and country) his response, which would also confirm the charge, would come resounding: *No, moi pas le pinaple!* More demonstrations of this bilingual et al confusion could also be found especially at hospitals and police stations." *Id*, at 172.

[147] *Id.* at 149-75.

[148] Benjamin, *supra*, note 46 at 126.

[149] *Supra*, note 46.

[150] *Supra*, note 82; & Harry Kuchah Kuchah, "From Bilingual Francophones to Bilingual Anglophones: The Role of

professor in Quebec confirmed this in 1976 by indicating that "several bilingual grammar schools were set up in the West but it was bilingualism for West Cameroon alone."[151]

The recent 2016 unintelligent and imperious imposition of the 'bilingualism in French' on the *lawyers* of 'West Cameroon' is actually what has plunged the country into its present impasse or war of independence. This appears to be the only time these self-seeking English-speaking lawyers could see anything wrong with it? The query is significant because, first, I aptly noted in 2016 that "the problems in Cameroon are often worsened by the fact that Cameroon's lawyers only talk human rights when their specific interests are in question; not bothering when the rights of other members of society are violated."[152] Second, we hear Dr Carlson Anyangwe too stating clearly in 1989 that,

although Cameroon is said to be an English-French bilingual country and the UNIYAO, on principle, a bilingual and bijural institution, the language of lecture [there] depends on whether the teacher talking the course is Francophone or Anglophone. In the final analysis, therefore, an English-speaking teacher teaches in English and a French-speaking teacher teaches in French. It is for the student to be bilingual so as to be able to follow classes in both languages. To teach law in the Yaoundé University therefore one

---

Teachers in the Rising 'Equities' of English-Medium Education in Cameroon", in E. Ushioda (ed.) *International Perspectives on Motivation. International Perspectives on English Language Teaching* (London: Palgrave Macmillan, 2013), 60.

[151] Frank M. Stark, "Federalism in Cameroon: The Shadow and the Reality" 10(3) *Canadian Journal of African Studies* (1976), 423-42 at 439.

[152] Cited in Fossungu, *supra*, note 1 at 168.

need not be bilingual, less still bi-jural. Indeed, most teachers in the Law Faculty are neither bilingual nor bijural at all.[153]

Writing about 'Language Confusion' as far back as 1998, some language rights critics could vividly "remember having chewed food that was not entirely mine some time ago. That was when I talked about the fate of our UNIBU [University of Buea] graduates in this country. Well, this time it's the story of those of their colleagues that have to go seeking for the Ngoa-lingual 'knowledge' over the Mungo River. More precisely, to our infamous Ngoa-Ekéllé which I hear is now Yaoundé N° 1? Certainly the N° 1 place for Anglophone misery in this country."[154] But how do the Anglophones themselves contribute to their misery? Quite an interesting query! Bilingualism (on the part of all students) could still have been possible, despite the disproportion in the number of Anglophone lecturers: provided the few of the English-speaking teachers held firm to the institution's unwritten teaching-language rule. But alas! These are the very people who – through wanting to be nice where being nice is anathema – work against bilingualism on the part of Francophone students (through the so-called *condensé*) and thereby belittle English at the UNIYAO and thereafter. These Anglophone lecturers constitute what Professor Anyangwe calls "the small number of teachers who either teach in both languages or who teach in one language and then give summaries in the other language."[155] As I

---

[153] Carlson Anyangwe, *The Magistracy and the Bar in Cameroon* (Yaoundé: PANAG-CEPER, 1989) at 203-204.

[154] Peter Areh-Afac Fossungu, "Language Confusion in Ngoa-Ekelle" *The Herald* N° 657 (7-8 September 1998), 4.

[155] *Supra*, note 153 at 204.

have ardently put it to these unthinking Anglophones, "Who is ever going to give you your language rights if you cannot stand tall and defend or impose them in glaring situations like these?"[156] The Francophone majority lecturers stick to the unwritten rule, being largely incapable of speaking English. In answering the question as to whether the student in the UNIYAO has got the right to answer questions in any of the country's official languages of his or her choice, Dr Anyangwe again has this to say:

There is no official university policy on this issue. And yet this is a crucial matter if only because there have been frequent cries, by students, of discrimination and victimisation on language grounds. If the constitution is anything to go by in this country then, courses should be offered in both English and French, questions set in both languages and the students free to do their assignments and answer examination questions in any of the two official languages of their choice.[157]

It should be noted that, in countries like Cameroon and Canada, bilingualism and bijuralism are often linked not only one to the other, but as well to the system of education. Legal translation is a different thing from legal bilingualism. The experts have generally argued forcefully against the claim "that bilingualism can [even] be realized by simply translating legal text."[158] In Cameroon, even such (English) translations are practically unavailable; and this regrettable fact finds its roots in Article 59 of

---

[156] Fossungu, *supra*, note 2 at 25.
[157] Anyangwe, *supra*, note 153 at 203.
[158] Macdonald, *supra*, note 6 at 119, & also 158-65.

the so-called Federal Constitution,[159] which expressly made only French the authentic language of the country. This Federal-Article 59 stance has been successively maintained in all the numerous and confusing Constitutions[160] until 1996: being the 1972 Constitution's Article 44; and the 1984 Constitution's Article 39. All this, of course, vividly contrasts with the language rights Sections (16-22) of the 1982 Canadian Constitution which clearly make both English and French versions of texts not only authentic but also of equal strength.[161] Has the 1996 Constitution changed anything at all in Cameroon?

---

[159] See *Loi N° 61-24 du 1er septembre 1961 portant révision constitutionnelle et tendant à adapter la constitution actuelle aux nécessités du Cameroun réunifié.*[hereinafter Federal Constitution]

[160] See 2 June 1972 Constitution of the United Republic of Cameroon (1972 Constitution); *Loi N° 84-1 du 4 février 1984*(1984 Constitution); and *Loi N° 91/001 du 23 avril portant modification des articles 5, 7, 8, 9, 26, 27 et 34 de la Constitution* (1991 Constitution).

[161] Further discussion of this Canadian formula is furnished by André Tremblay, "Les droits linguistiques", in G-A. Beaudoin et E.P. Mendes (eds.), *Charte canadienne des droits et libertés* 3ᵉ édition (Montréal: Wilson et Lafleur Ltée, 1996), 901; G. Jourdain, "Redonner vie au bilinguisme de l'administration de la justice au pays de Louis Riel" 1(2) *Revue de la Common Law* (1997), 169; T. Scassa, "Langue et justice: la transformation du droit" 1(2) *Revue de la Common Law* (1997), 247; and Olivier Nguyen, *Document de jurisprudence concernant des droits linguistiques garantis par la Charte canadienne des droits et libertés* (no city: PADL – Programme d'appui aux droits linguistiques, 2013).

Post-1996 Bilingualism: Rejecting Swisselgianism and Promotion of Indigenous Languages

There are some claims that the bilingualism situation has since changed with the arrival of the 1996 Constitution which conspicuously claims in its opening Article: (1) the constitutionalization of official bilingualism; (2) the making of both English and French versions of the Constitution of equal *status* (though whether or not this includes their *authenticity*, is not clear); and (3) that "The State shall guarantee the promotion of [this constitutionalized official] bilingualism *throughout* the country... [and also] will endeavour to protect and promote national languages."[162] It can thus be seen that Article 1(3) of "This law [which] shall be registered and published in the Official Gazette of the Republic of Cameroon in English and French and implemented as the Constitution of the Republic of Cameroon"[163] flatly rejects the Belgian and Swiss Strict Territorial Principles, better known as Swisselgianism. Again, unlike its predecessors which always put 'in French and English', this 1996 Constitution seems to have significantly followed the alphabetical rule – a rule often adhered to where no subordination is intended. Let me properly demonstrate this vital rule with some questionable and colonially-inspired definition of continent.

The Great Language Puzzle and Nwangong-Zoomitionism: What is Continental in the Definition of Continent?

---

[162] 1996 Constitution, *supra*, note 41, Article 1(3) (emphasis added).
[163] *Id,* Article 69.

Just hear the Just Lecture (who is seen in Figure #5) who was '*Just Announcing Just the Unknown in Just African Civilization*' to better understand some strangers to Africa. With my proper substitution of 'Bangwa' with 'African', Mamie Regina's lecture to the meek city teacher in early 1984 (if my translation of the Bangwa language is good enough) would appear to go on like this:

> If I just open this Lecture by just telling you that Africans are just the most intelligently civilized people on the planet, some of you may just think that I am just saying so just because I am African. But, just not to just send you to just go and just study the lengthy Science of Death, just how many *just* do you have in there already? Seven or Ten you just said? Are we told that there are just five or how many continents? I just don't know who just might be just correct but just distribute those 'just' to them. And if there is just a real shortage then just add the 'just' that are just still needed just on your own. In case of excess (as there just must be), then you just *Europeanly* and *Rational-Choicely* make unjust profit with the rest. Hey! This is just surely not a Just Lecture in the eyes of some who just always just want it only their unjust way. But you are just entitled to just think what you may about the just thesis just proffered just as its just author is just entitled to just put it forward.....[164]

---

[164] Regina Akiefac Fossungu, private communication, February 1984.

Figure #5: Mafor Regina Akiefac Fossungu
Source: Photo taken by Momany Fossungu

I do not need to remind readers that these are Africans who have never set foot in the postcolonial educational classroom! In this particular lecture of hers Mamie Regina was obviously also wondering about the number of continents in the world, among other lielistical philosophical theories. Listening to experts like her then, crisebacologists would quickly realize we need to address some important issues, such as: Is there a continent called Asia that is apart from what is known as Europe? How is 'troublesome' Russia (to Americans, that is) in Europe and we are still being told that China is in Asia when those two countries share frontier in the same continent? 'A Lot of Bullshit,' says the old Nwangong woman called Mamie Regina, aka The Just Lecturer. That is quite right, if readers also ask my fossungupalogistic or frantalkist view that is sufficiently grounded in the works of so-called experts, the same lielisticalists for that matter. Tell Nwangongers, for instance, like the God-badifying Virginia colour-continentalizing judge, that there are 'Malay Europeans', 'Red Europeans', and 'Yellow Europeans'.[165] Or, still *stupidly*, that we have 'East- and Asian-Europeans': Mohandas Karamchand Gandhi, the revered leader of India's freedom movement (described as a stark racist by two South African University professors) would seem to be propagating a theory like this when, in an open letter to the Natal Parliament in 1893, Gandhi wrote:

> I venture to point out that both the English and the Indians spring from a common stock, called the Indo-Aryan. ... A general belief seems to prevail in the Colony that the Indians are little better, if at all, than savages or the Natives of Africa. Even the children are taught to believe in that manner, with the result that the Indian is being dragged down to the position of a raw Kaffir.[166]

---

[165] See Fossungu, *supra*, note 110 at 33.

[166] Akoh Asa'na, "What Indian Independence Leader Thought about Black People" @ https://www.washingtonpost.com/news/worldviews/wp/2015/09/03/what-did-mahatma-gandhi-think-of-black-people/ [as sent to SobaAmerica@yahoogroups.com by Akoh Asa'na on September 26, 2015 at 9.26 AM].

You can tell Ambazonia's Nwangongers all of that cockshit! BUT just don't even venture around the Fondom of Nwangong with this lielistical talk of your Europe and your Asia being two different continents: because your own very definition starkly contradicts your theory. Sara Hawker and Maurice Waite are dictionaristic specialists who inform us in their 'most trusted dictionary'[167] that a continent is: "**1** any of the world's main continuous expanses of land (Europe, Asia, Africa, North and South America, Australia, Antarctica). **2 (the Continent)** the mainland of Europe, as distinct from the British Isles."[168] According to them, therefore, we have six continents that they separate with their commas. As argued by some, this is supposed to be accepted docilely because of the poverty of "innovation and creativity that is imparted by the inherited system of education";[169] all springing from the exclusion of philosophy in curricula, especially in British colonies. Refusing to be under the yoke of colonial education (like Mamie Regina and Fon David Foncha Fossungu obviously do), 'Tesizoomed-Eyed'[170] crisebacologists have the following few observations.

---

[167] Sara Hawker and Maurice Waite, *Oxford Paperback Dictionary & Thesaurus* 2nd edition (Oxford: Oxford University Press, 2007).

[168] *Id.* at 190 (bold is original).

[169] Gwaravanda, *supra*, note 118 at 255.

[170] Reacting to the August 2019 publication of this writer's book on human rights and the judiciary in Africa, Maitre Peterson Tesi (a Toronto-based lawyer of African origin) wrote: "Waoooh. You are a head. You see not just with a large eye but zoomed eyes. I have respect for you in that you talk and you produce. How many people especially with the controversies in our country show this type of x-ray and say or contribute their thoughts into what has to be done? I will say you are one among a few resilient ones. I was on

Firstly, the definers are unnecessarily Eurocentric in not respecting the famous alphabetical rule that obviously accords Africa the first mention, followed by the other '*As*' in order before getting to the lone E and lone N. No doubt that Professor Artwell Nhemachena of the University of Namibia has ably theorised in 2018 about the 'World Not Being Humanistic Enough to Listen to Afrikan Voices'.[171] That also includes excluding African languages. As Marongwe and Mawere can also help to state it, these definers unambiguously "are partial, Eurocentric, [and] are inclined to force a lopsided understanding of human rights and they distort lived experiences especially in Third World countries."[172] I am here solidifying the point on Third Worlders, going through progressively by having the next point of (dis)interest.

Secondly, can these 'God-badifying' Eurocentrists exactly demonstrate to us how Europe and (most of their) Asia *are* not a 'main continuous expanse of land'? They just cannot because they are just bent on just creating a Eurocentric colour-assigning mirror just for everyone, just leading to Quijano's theorization that "when

---

my way from court when I got the message. I opened and checked. It is who you are. Looking forward to read this. It should be worth it." (Peterson Tesi, private communication, 13 August 2019).

[171] Artwell Nhemachena, "World Not Humanistic Enough to Listen to Afrikan Voices" available at: https://www.unisa.ac.za/sites/corporate/default/Colleges/Human-Sciences/News-&-events/Articles/World-not-humanistic-enough-to-listen-to-Afrikan-voices2018.

[172] Ngonidzashe Marongwe and Tinashe Mawere, "Mandela and Coloniality in South Africa", in Munyaradzi Mawere and Tendal Rinos Mwanaka (eds.), *Democracy, Good Governance and Development in Africa* (Bamenda: Langaa RPCIG, 2015), 125-55 at 137.

we look in our Eurocentric mirror, the image that we see is not composite but also necessarily partial and distorted. The tragedy is that we have all been led, knowingly or not, wanting it or not, to see and accept that image as our own and as belonging to us alone. In this way, we continue being what we are not."[173] This small book highly reflects on and condemns vehemently the idea in the last sentence particularly, calling on Africans especially to wake up from lielisticalism and live proudly as Africans! The magnification or zooming of the lielisticalism is meant to aid toward these goals, bringing me to the next point to be zoomed.

Thirdly, how would the British Isles be in the European continent whereas these and that 'mainland' would not be a 'continuous expanse of land'? That uncontroverted contradiction just necessarily requires the rewriting of straightforward or foureyesismatic dictionaries by objective minds: since, to just get straightforward schooling again and again and again from just Nelson Mandela, the world's problems are largely caused by people who are not objective, those who view issues only from the standpoint of just their own interests. That injustice is precisely what they then try to nicely cover up by calling it Rational Choice. Where did they hide the *IR* before it? Get it back where it rightly and truthfully belongs! Mandela's incisive point has also been exemplified above by the stalled adoption of an indigenous common language in Cameroon, a country where those who dislike straight-shooting have been instructed to hurry to because it is the best place in the world they would easily find bottles into which to cork themselves away from the truth.[174] It is just time, therefore,

---

[173] *Id.* at 138.
[174] See Fossungu, *supra*, note 94 at 80.

the window is just shown to these lielisticalists or corner-kickers just like Miss Douala's unjust marriage. *Married* when you do not desire the supposedly poor local stranger but *unmarried* when you realize you so badly desire his hard currency: dollars![175]

Talking of American dollars smoothly brings us back to the Constitution which is so adored and upheld by Americans, very unlike Cameroonians. Leaving the vexed issue of the yet-to-be-promoted promotion of national languages aside, Cameroon's Bilingualism Throughout the Country (BTC) thus firmly says NO to Swisselgianism, appearing to instead lean towards the Canadian *Charter* goals of Uniform Bilingualism Across the Country or Ubackism. I would gravely doubt that Canadian identification though because, looked at closely, the Cameroonian modus operandi would appear to be promoting only what some critics have castigated as being 'bilingual in French' or as 'Ngoalingualism'. One does not need to go to heaven to find evidence for the assertion of those language policy experts. First, there is the commendation of the 1996 Constitution's Article 69 made some moments ago. That alphabetical-praise of the 1996 apparent change can only be valid to a person who only reads the 'inauthentic' English version because the 'authentic' French version still talks of "*La presente loi sera enregistrée et publiée au Journal Officiel de la République du Cameroun en francais et en anglais…*"[176] *A* always comes before *F* in the alphabet, whether in the English or French languages.

The plausibility of the 'bilingualism in French' thesis is also plainly seen, even without reading glasses, in the infamous 'Green-Red-Yellow Cover Story' from one of Cameroon's

---

[175] *Id.* at 115-16.
[176] *Supra*, note 163.

uncompromising language politics experts who (in theorizing on 'Ngoalingualism' while 'Mocking the Bijuralism and Bilingualism Birds') declared in September 1998 that "to gain time and space by shortening the lengthy Much Ado About Nothing", he would simply invite any doubting Mary to the Green-Red-Yellow Cover [of the 1984 Constitution] where she would be flabbergasted to find that, on the portion supposedly to be the English version (Constitution of the Republic of Cameroon), she can identify all our ten provinces – assuming [of course] that she is at all Ngoalingual – only in French: *Province de L'Extreme Nord, Province du Nord, Province de L'Adamaoua, Province du Nord-Ouest, Province de L'Ouest, Province du Sud-Ouest, Province du Littoral, Province du Centre, Province de L'Est*, and *Province Du Sud*. Ngoalingualism, isn't it?[177]

To yet other critics, there is only the flattering strategy in all the talk of bilingualism in Cameroon. This is the case of Ephraim Inoni who was the Assistant Secretary-General at the presidency of the Cameroon Republic. During the award of certificates to final year students of the Bamenda Linguistic Centre, Inoni "termed the Northwest the citadel of Bilingualism in Cameroon, noting that French was being taught in CPC [Cameroon Protestant College] Bali long before the former Southern Cameroons joined *La République du Cameroun.*"[178] Bilingualism in Cameroon is thus merely another advanced name for assimilation of the English-speaking minority; explaining why it has taken the raging Ambazonian War of Liberation for cosmetic things like the so-

---

[177] Cited in Fossungu, *supra*, note 2 at 171-72 (italics used to replace original capitals).

[178] Kini Nsom, "Inoni Woos Northwesterners" *The Post* (Limbe, 8 May 1998), 3.

called Bilingualism Commission to be calculatedly created in 2020. Otherwise, it is hard to explain the achievements of Foumban, including the institutionalization of unfettered appointments of even West Cameroon's prime minister (now called governors/regional delegates who are most often not even Anglophones[179]) by the automatic 'federal' unilingual president.

The unilingualism of Cameroonian officials contrasts vividly with Canada, Belgium, and (former) White South Africa, where some form of bilingualism is not only encouraged among the educated elites, but has been made a condition for entry into and advancing in the middle and upper reaches of the government bureaucracy. It is even regarded as a necessary and decidedly

---

[179] "When we collectively allow the crooked-voice guy there in the Etoudi Palace to single-handedly appoint the V-Cs and *Recteurs* (to limit just to these here) and then turn around and expect such appointed officials to act as if they have a free hand, then I say we are all *nosifeans*. People with no schooling in four-eyesism, is what it means. *Hisofeans* [like HRM Fon DF Fossungu and Mafor Regina Akiefac Fossungu, for example] would not be pinning the problems on Nalova and Teresa Akenji (to stay west of the Mungo River). They would rather be fighting to have universities in this country run as autonomous bodies by the localities. And that cannot be limited to those academic institutions alone, since a university cannot be autonomously run by an entity that is not itself autonomous. That position would be no different from saying that the current governors of the regions (call them whatever you will) do in fact manage said entities. *Lie-lie!* Governors must be duly elected by the inhabitants of their various regions for that to effectively happen. How to make all that reality is already outlined in the TRILOGY OF GOVERNANCE [that] Momany has humbly brought forth and is here challenging us all to utilize to bring our people out of the *Quagmaticking* wilderness and into the Promised Land." Cited in Fossungu, *supra*, note 85 at 153 (original emphasis & square brackets).

advantageous factor for anyone entertaining high political aspirations.[180] This is only normal because in multilingual (or bilingual) polities language plays an enormous role in politics and education. Some experts do regard Canada's Sections 16-20 as "focus[ing] on the language of government, and s.23 [as] concerning the language of education."[181] All this, one could think, has been possible in these other countries mostly because the voter counts in them. Where elections mean absolutely nothing, as in Cameroon, language will only be an apt centralizing instrument in the hands of the ones who make the unfettered appointments. In such a system, all the talk of cultural dualism is bound to be mere unhelpful rhetoric, capped, of course, by confusion. After a very elaborate survey of 'Language Politics in Post-Colonial Africa', a prominent member of the Presidential Advisory Committee in Abuja, Nigeria, reached the inevitable conclusion in 1997 that:

> Ambivalence would seem to characterize the language policies of post-colonial African states. Most of their national constitutions certainly took note of the existing 'babel' in their respective states; hence the nationalists voluntarily adopted their colonial linguistic heritage. That accounts for why all Commonwealth African countries

---

[180] Yosef Israel Goell, *Bi-Nationalism and Bi-Lingualism in Three Modernized States: A Comparative Study of Canada, Belgium, and White South Africa* (PhD Dissertation, Columbia University, University Microfilms International, 1978) at 338-40.

[181] Iacabucci, *supra*, note 49 at 95.

(except for Tanzania and now Cameroon and Mozambique) adopted English as their official/national language.[182]

---

[182] Cited in Fossungu, *supra*, note 2 at 164-65.

LANGUAGE LESSONS OF GLOBAVILLAGISM AND CLOSING REMARKS

The concept of *globavillagism* derives from one of my books and I use it to describe a rare genre of open-mindedness and foresight.[183] The closing passage of the previous chapter is from post-1996 writings, meaning that the camouflage of bilingualism in Cameroon seems not to be fooling a lot of people. The critics of 'bilingualism in French' are correct and I have personally had to listen to the experiences of some English-speaking Cameroonians (who have studied in Quebec's French-speaking institutions) that would speak volumes to the blinkeredness of their French-speaking compatriots. Even at these Quebec French-speaking universities, Cameroon's Francophones are having lots of problems since almost all the study materials are in English. Welcome to Northern North America! While in their small world of Cameroon they often boasted about having absolutely nothing to do with *la langue de la minorité*, completely oblivious that their African Cameroon and its 'Mother France' or the European Cameroon are very insignificant portions of the globe. The European-Cameroon description of France is coming from 'the Two-Cameroon Theory'.[184]

"It's hard", according to the Gazette Editorial with which one cannot easily disagree, "to see why anyone, except the most narrow-minded, could get so upset at the prospect of young people being fluently bilingual, or trilingual in the case of immigrant

---

[183] Fossungu, *supra*, note 127 at x-xii.
[184] Fossungu, *supra*, note 5 at 163-68.

children."[185] Such narrow-mindedness is magnified in view of Quebec's status (within a 'uniformly bilingual' Canada) and geography (the North American English-dominating continent). It is the same for Cameroon, in view of its privileged but unexploited situation on the African continent and the world at large. Young people must be encouraged these days to 'Become International-minded'[186] because the world is fast becoming what some cultural experts now call a Global Village. What is there to prevent United Afrika from also becoming a Global Village to Afrikans with the aid of Swisselgianism? I think the entire assimilation or 'bilingualism in French' policy is not only obnoxious to the concept of justice but also brilliantly exposes the feeblemindedness of its promoters. My theories in 'Language Confusion in Cameroon' better tell the story of the proliferation of 'écoles bilingues' in West Cameroon that has instead created a 'confusion language'. "As concerns the so-called *Francanglais*", I have asserted, "one will easily hear in students' discussions sentences like '*Mon papa say je peux go et spend les vacances for Victoria. But je ne go pas because il ne m'a pas give le transport.*' And this, mark you, concerns students of all levels. On which side are we in this country? Are we Ngoa-lingual, Francanglais or simply in Confusion?"[187] As a sort of response to the troubling quiz, readers are schooled to the effect that:

> The confusion called *Francanglais* is now not only growing at an alarming rate; but it jeopardizes, as well, even the so-

---

[185] Gazette Editorial, "Bilingualism is No Threat" *Montreal Gazette* (29 January 1997), B2.
[186] Ikeda, *supra*, note 72 at 51-54.
[187] Fossungu, *supra*, note 154.

called master language that is meant to be propagated. Could this be a clear case of shooting one's own foot? The alarming growth of such confusion has been given impetus by the proliferation of so-called *écoles bilingues* which would appear to observers to be clearly of ambiguous value for economic, social and political development. That language, I think, would rather be better preserved and spread in a Swiss-type territorially-run Cameroon than what is actually the case. It is not hard to see how that is so (considering the Anglophone-Francophone population/territorial ratios), although those concerned would not – despite all their claims to monopoly of knowledge. And all what that knowledge would appear to entail could end only with their irreplaceable New Ethnic Group that has to create morons out of people.[188]

Could the preference of this confusion by the Cameroonian authorities be their simplistic way of avoiding the danger inherent in Harry Kuchah's findings on the preference of Anglophone education system, if Swisselgianism becomes the rule in Cameroon? The University of Bath (United Kingdom) professor has interestingly attempted to explain why English-medium (Anglophone) education is fast becoming the coveted medium of education for many Francophone children in Cameroon in spite of the existence of complex language ideologies and attitudes that represent Anglophones and 'anglophonism' as second class in a country dominated by Francophones and a political system that is

---

[188] *Ibid.*

hugely borrowed from, and influenced by, France.[189] The question here assumes added importance in view of the expibasketical theory of an experienced educationist, indicating that,

having taught in both 'systems' of education in Cameroon for a couple of years, I have had several opportunities to listen to French-speaking students' admiration and yearning for the '*système anglophone.*' But they are condemned to live with what they do not like simply because parochialism on the part of the leaders would not permit 'copying' from *la minorité*, in spite of the great harm that not doing so brings to young French-speaking Cameroonians.[190]

Further examples of some of 'the great harm' I have alluded to, are from Harry Kuchah who has demonstrated that the 'From Bilingual Francophones to Bilingual Anglophones' trend that is generally in the offing in Sub-Sahara Africa is "often confounded in a country like Cameroon where the language of instruction presents a barrier to parental involvement in education for children whose parents are not educated in the language of their schooling."[191] Swisselgianism, I must submit persistently, could greatly remedy this situation confronting Cameroon's (Africa's) 'leaders of tomorrow' (a tomorrow that is never coming though), as well as promoting national-continental unity. Because both parent and child here would be fluent in the language of the region they are in, or simply move elsewhere if that is not agreeable to them. Therefore, rather than attempting to deceive people with their unsavoury and dishonest 'uniform bilingualism across the country',

---

[189] Kuchah, *supra*, note 150 at 60.
[190] Fossungu, *supra*, note 140 at 135 (original emphasis, note omitted).
[191] Kuchah, *supra*, note 82.

Cameroon and Canada should better go to Europe and ask for the honest metrics of Swisselgianism. That is straightforward multilingual language policy that works excellently for both national unity and human rights respect. This is now an imperative for Cameroon especially because (as evidenced by the Ambazonia-LRC war that is ongoing) the younger generation of English-speaking Cameroonians can no longer swallow the assimilation and discriminatory second-class-citizen pills, appearing now to be solely and solidly going by the following advice and encouragement I, as a human rights activist, gave them in 1998:

> As I said before, it is now left to you, students or youths, to teach these our old guards that their epoch is long gone and that, therefore, they have to desist from trying to continue encumbering your lifestyle of today and tomorrow with their defunct mode of thinking of the dark sixties. I have trust that the young people of this Second Home country are sapient enough to be able to realize that. Would the G.C.E. Affair not have proven your capacity to by-pass these jokers and take control of what affects your own life? More power to your elbows![192]

That power to the elbows of the youths is obviously being greatly enhanced with the freedom and judicial independence strategies in my book on judicial politics and other techniques for *Getting Africa out of the Dungeon*, a prison being perpetuated by the traitor mentality which I think this book has also so beautifully dissected (though not as well as my next book will do). What is being advocated as

---

[192] Fossungu, *supra*, note 42.

being needed in the multicultural polities in question, it must be emphasized, is not the abandonment of any rights to have any of their (foreign) languages/legal systems for all purposes. The advocacy is simply for an attempt by Cameroonians in particular and Africans generally to become multilingual/multijural in the semantics of each other's rights-valuation, with Swisselgianism potentially promoting this better than the other formulae. This is not impossible because "it really is possible to see things – even the most concrete things – simultaneously yet differently; and that seeing simultaneously yet differently is more easily done by two people than one; but that one person can get the hang of it with lots of time and effort."[193] Canada, no doubt, has been making a lot of effort, albeit not as radically as some people would have liked. But is this what has also availed in Cameroon? Have people in Cameroon put in such time and effort? Or is effort even being made to see respect for human rights (including the cultural and linguistic) happen there? With the war that is raging on, is the country then actually showing proof that it can lead the continent in Getting Africa into Africa for Africans? Is Ambazonia then breaking away in order to free and unite Africa?

---

[193] Williams, *supra*, note 13 at 410-11; also see Maneli, *supra*, note 9 at 22, 23 & 48.

REFERENCES

Ajulo, Sunday B. (1997) "Myth and Reality of Law, Language and International Organization in Africa: The Case of African Economic Community" 41(1) *Journal of African Law*, 27-42.

Allnutt, Alan (1999) "Challenging the Orthodoxy of Bill 101" *Montreal Gazette* (20 March), B5.

Anchimbe, Eric A. (2013) *Language Policy and Identity Construction: The Dynamics of Cameroon's Multilingualism* (Amsterdam: John Benjamins Publishing Company).

Anyangwe, Carlson (1989) *The Magistracy and the Bar in Cameroon* (Yaoundé: PANAG-CEPER).

Anyefru, Emmanuel (2011) 'The Refusal to Belong: Limits of the Discourse on Anglophone Nationalism in Cameroon" 28(2) *The Journal of Third World Studies*, 277-306.

_____(2010) "Paradoxes of Internationalization of the Anglophone Problem in Cameroon" 28(1) *Journal of Contemporary African Studies*, 85-101.

Asa'na, Akoh (2015) "What Indian Independence Leader Thought about Black People" @ https://www.washingtonpost.com/news/worldviews/wp/2015/09/03/what-did-mahatma-gandhi-think-of-black-people/ [as sent to SobaAmerica@yahoogroups.com by Akoh Asa'na on September 26, 2015 at 9.26 AM].

Asante, Richard (2015) "The State and Knowledge of Democracy in West Africa: A Critical Analysis", in Munyaradzi Mawere and Tendai Rinos Mwanaka (eds.), *Democracy, Good Governance and Development in Africa* (Bamenda: Langaa RPCIG), 157-92.

Atanga, Mufor (2011) *The Anglophone Cameroon Predicament* (Bamenda Langaa RPCIG).

Authier, Philip (1996) "Bouchard Calls for Tolerance: Economy First" *Montreal Gazette* (23 November), A1.

Bayefsky, Anne F. (1989) *Canada's Constitution Act 1982 and Amendments* Vol. 1 (Toronto: McGraw-Hill Ryerson).

Beng, Peter Ngea (1997) "Ministers Shy Away from Public Functions As Cabinet Reshuffle Fears Intensify" *The Herald* (Yaoundé, 1-2 December), 1-2.

Benjamin, Jacques (1972) *Les camerounais occidentaux: la minorité dans un état bicommunautaire* (Montréal: Université de Montréal).

Biya, Paul (1986) *Communal Liberalism* (London: Macmillan).

Bjornson, Richard (1991) *The African Quest for Freedom and Identity: Cameroonian Writing and the National Experience* (Bloomington & Indianapolis: Indiana University Press).

Bram, C.M.B. (1989) "The Terminology of Babel: A Suggestion" 19(2) *Journal of West African Languages*, 125-27.

Cullen, Richard (1990) "Adaptive Federalism in Belgium" 13 *University of New South Wales Law Journal*, 346-58/

Das, Satya (1996) "Playing by the Rules in Indonesia: A Little Homework Goes a Long Way for Investors" *The Edmonton Journal* (26 December), E1.

David, Michel (1999) "Francophones Outside Quebec Pose Problem" *Montreal Gazette* (10 December), B3.

Davidson, Basil (1991) *Africa in History: Themes and Outlines* rev. & exp. ed. (New York: Macmillan).

Dias, R.W.M. (1976) *Jurisprudence* 4th edition (London: Butterworth).

Dicklitch, Susan (2011) "The Southern Cameroons and Minority Rights in Cameroon" 29(1) *Journal of Contemporary African Studies*, 49-62.

Douthat, Ross (2016) "The Dangers of Hillary Clinton" @ http://www.nytimes.com/2016/10/23/opinion/sunday/the-dangers-of-hillary-clinton.html?ref=opinion&_r=

Ebai, S.E. (2009) "The Right to Self-Determination and the Anglophone Cameroon Situation" 13(5) *The International Journal of Human Rights*, 631-53.

Eko, Lyonga (2003) "The English-Language Press and the 'Anglophone Problem' in Cameroon: Group Identity, Culture, and the Politics of Nostalgia" 20(1) *Journal of Third World Studies*, 79-102.

Etchu, George and Allan W. Grundstorm (1999) *Official Bilingualism and Linguistic Communication in Cameroon-Bilinguisme officiel et communication linguistique au Cameroun* (New York: P. Lang).

Fonchingong, Charles C. (2005) "Exploring the Politics of Identity and Ethnicity in State Reconstruction in 'Democratic' Cameroon" 11(4) *Social Identities*, 363-80.

Forbin, Boniface (1998) "Herald Editorial – Nsam Disaster: Government is still Owing" *The Herald* (Yaoundé, 3-4 August), 4.

Forsey, Eugene (1989) *How Canadians Govern Themselves* (2nd edition, 1988), in G.P. Van Nes, *The Structure of Federalism*, 7.

Fossungu, Peter Ateh-Afac (2021) *Family Law and Politics with Biology and Royalty in Africa and North America* (Chitungwiza, Zimbabwe: Mwanaka Media and Publishing).

_____ (2018) *Historical and Partyological Postponement of Democracy in Canada: Elongating the Business Pleasure War in Africa?* (Saarbrucken, Germany: LAP Lambert Academic Publishers).

_____ (2018) "Political Naivety, Corruption, and Poverty Promotion in Africa: Riding the 'Poorest-ugliest French' Bijuralism Horse from Cameroon to Canada via Britain", in Munyaradzi Mawere (ed.), *The Political Economy of Poverty, Vulnerability and Disaster Risk Management: Building Bridges of Resilience, Entrepreneurship and Development in Africa's 21st Century* (Bamenda: Langaa RPCIG), 123-73.

_____ (2015) *Africans and Negative Competition in Canadian Factories: Revamping Canada's Immigration, Employment and Welfare Policies?* (Bamenda: Langaa RPCIG).

_____ (2015) "African Democracy vis-a-vis Western Democracy: Afrikenticating, Follyfying, Expibasketizing, and Reversing the 'African Democracy' Debate", in Munyaradzi Mawere and Tendai Rinos Mwanaka (eds.), *Democracy, Good Governance and Development in Africa* (Bamenda: Langaa RPCIG), 71-124.

_____ (2015) *Family Politics and Deception in Northern North America and West-Central Africa: Litigating God's Marriage Intention?* (Bamenda: Langaa RPCIG).

_____ (2015) *The HISOFE Dictionary of Midnight Politics: Expibasketical Theories on Afrikentication and African Unity* (Bamenda: Langaa RPCIG).

_____ (2014) *Africa's Anthropological Dictionary on Love and Understanding: Marriage and the Tensions of Belonging in Cameroon* (Bamenda: Langaa RPCIG).

_____ (2013) *Africans in Canada: Blending Canadian and African Lifestyles?* (Bamenda: Langaa RPCIG).

_____ (2013) *Democracy and Human Rights in Africa: The Politics of Collective Participation and Governance in Cameroon* (Bamenda: Langaa RPCIG).

_____ (2013) *Understanding Confusion in Africa: The Politics of Multiculturalism and Nation-building in Cameroon* (Bamenda: Langaa RPCIG).

_____ (1999) "When Will Cameroonians Ever Grow Up?" *The Herald* (Yaoundé, 20-21 July), 19.

_____ (1998) "Language Confusion in Ngoa-Ekelle" *The Herald* N° 657 (7-8 September), 4.

_____ (1998) "Paradoxes of Cameroon's Intellectuals" *The Herald* (Yaoundé, 16-18 January), 4.

_____ (1998) "Revisiting 'My Second Home'" *The Herald* (Yaoundé, 26-27 August), 10.

Gazette Editorial (1997) "Bilingualism is No Threat" *Montreal Gazette* (29 January), B2.

Frye, Northrop (1986) "Language as the Home of Human Life", in Michael Owen (ed.), *Salute to Scholarship: Essays Presented at the Official Opening of Athabasca University* (Athabasca, Alberta: Athabasca University), 20-33.

Goell, Yosef Israel (1978) *Bi-Nationalism and Bi-Lingualism in Three Modernized States: A Comparative Study of Canada, Belgium, and White South Africa* (PhD Dissertation, Columbia University, University Microfilms International).

Gold, Marc (1985) "The Mask of Objectivity: Politics and Rhetoric in the Supreme Court of Canada" 7 *Supreme Court Review*, 455.

Green, William (1999) "Schools, Signs, and Separation: Quebec Anglophones, Canadian Constitutional Politics, and International Language Rights" 27 *Denver Journal of International Law and Policy*, 449.

Gwaravanda, Ephraim Taurai (2018) "The Impoverished African and the Poverty of Colonially Inherited Education in Africa", in Munyaradzi Mawere (ed.), *The Political Economy of Poverty, Vulnerability and Disaster Risk Management: Building Bridges of Resilience, Entrepreneurship and Development in Africa's 21st Century* (Bamenda: Langaa RPCIG), 255-77.

Hawker, Sara and Maurice Waite (2007) *Oxford Paperback Dictionary & Thesaurus* 2nd edition (Oxford: Oxford University Press).

Iacobucci, Frank (1994) "Judicial Review by the Supreme Court of Canada under the Charter of Rights and Freedoms: The First Ten Years", in David M. Beatty (ed.), *Human Rights and Judicial Review – A Comparative Perspective* (Dordrecht: Martinus Nijhoff Publishers), 93-134.

Ikeda, Daikasu (1987) *A Lasting Peace* Vol. II (New York & Tokyo: Weatherhill).

Johnson, Douglas H. (2013) "New Sudan or South Sudan? The Multiple Meanings of Self-Determination in Sudan's Comprehensive Peace Agreement" 15(2) *Civil Wars*, 141-56.

Johnson, Willard R. (1970) *The Cameroon Federation: Political Integration in a Fragmentary Society* (Princeton, N.J.: Princeton University Press).

Jourdain, Guy (1997) "Redonner vie au bilinguisme de l'administration de la justice au pays de Louis Riel" 1(2) *Revue de la Common Law*, 169.

Kagan, Robert (2016) "Why We Shouldn't Forgive the Republicans Who Sold Their Souls" @ https/www.washingtonpost.com/opinions/the-cowardly-gop-has-engineered-its-own-suicide/2016/10/11/ec585af8-8f22-11e6a3-d500

Kondaks, Tony (1998) "Liberals Were as Bad for Anglos as the PQ" *Montreal Gazette* (15 December), B2.

Konings, Piet (1999) "The Anglophone Struggle for Federalism in Cameroon", in L.R. Basita and J. Ibrahim (eds.), *Federalism and Decentralization in Africa: The Multiethnic Challenge* (Fribourg Institut du Fédéralisme,), 289-325.

Konings, Piet and Francis B. Nyamnjoh (1997) "The Anglophone Problem in Cameroon" 35(2) *The Journal of Modern African Studies*, 207-29.

Kuchah, Harry Kuchah (2017) "Early English Medium Instruction in Francophone Cameroon: The Injustice of Equal Opportunity" @ www.academia.edu/34773512/Kuchah_Kuchah_2017 _Early_English_medium_instruction_in_Francophone _Cameroon_Pre_publication_version.

_____ (2013) "From Bilingual Francophones to Bilingual Anglophones: The Role of Teachers in the Rising 'Equities' of English-Medium Education in Cameroon", in E. Ushioda (ed.) *International Perspectives on Motivation. International Perspectives on English Language Teaching* (London: Palgrave Macmillan), 60.

LaSalle (2010) "2010 Moulins d'Or Community Award: Fidelis Folifac" @ www.http.ville.montreal.qu.ca/pls/portal/docs/page/a rrond_1st_en/media/document/folefac.

Le Vine, Victor T. (1986) "Political-Cultural Schizophrenia in Francophone Africa", in I.J. Mowoe and Richard Bjornson (eds.), *Africa and the West: The Legacies of Empires* (New York: Greenwood Press), 159-73.

Liebich, André (1996) "Federalism Swiss Style" *McGill News* (Alumni Quarterly), 11.

Macdonald, Roderick A. (1997) "Legal Bilingualism" 42 *McGill Law Journal* 119-167.

Maneli, Mieczyslaw (1994) *Perelman's New Rhetoric as Philosophy and Methodology for the Next Century* (Dordrecht: Kluwer Academic Publishers).

Marongwe, Ngonidzashe and Tinashe Mawere (2015) "Mandela and Coloniality in South Africa", in Munyaradzi Mawere and Tendal Rinos Mwanaka (eds.), *Democracy, Good Governance and Development in Africa* (Bamenda: Langaa RPCIG), 125-55.

Marsh, David (2010) "Meta-Theoretical Issues", in David Marsh and Gerry Stoker (eds.), *Theory and Methods in Political Science* 3rd edition (London: Palgrave Macmillan), 212-31.

Mawere, Munyaradzi, Annastasia M. Mawere and Pedro Celso Jovo (2015) "Culture, Ethics and Politics for a Better and Sustainable Africa: The Mozambican Experience", in Munyaradzi Mawere and Tendai Rinos Mwanaka (eds.), *Democracy, Good Governance and Development in Africa* (Bamenda: Langaa RPCIG), 269-95.

Mbaku, John Mokum (2018) *Protecting Minority Rights in African Countries: A Constitutional Political Economy Approach* (Cheltenham, UK: Edward Elgar Publishing Ltd.).

Mbuagbo, Oben Timothy (2002) "Cameroon: Exploiting Anglophone Identity in State Deconstruction" 8(3) *Social Identities*, 431-38.

Mohr, J.W. (1993) "From Saussure to Derida: Margins of Law" 18 *Queen's Law Journal*, 343-79.

Nhemachena, Artwell (2018) "World Not Humanistic Enough to Listen to Afrikan Voices" available at: https://www.unisa.ac.za/sites/corporate/default/Coll

eges/Human-Sciences/News-&-events/Articles/World-not-humanistic-enough-to-listen-to-Afrikan-voices.

Newman, Peter C. (1968) *The Canadian Establishment* Volume 1 (Toronto: McClelland and Stewart Limited).

Ngefac, Aloysius (2010) "Linguistic Choices in Postcolonial Multilingual Cameroon" 19(3) *Nordic Journal of African Studies*, 149-64.

Nguyen, Olivier (2013) *Document de jurisprudence concernant des droits linguistiques garantis par la Charte canadienne des droits et libertés* (no city: PADL – Programme d'appui aux droits linguistiques).

Ngwafor, Aldarin (1998) "Urgent Need for a Law School in Cameroon" *The Herald* (Yaoundé, 12-14 June), 4.

Nsom, Kini (1998) "Inoni Woos Northwesterners" *The Post* (Limbe, 8 May), 3.

NYT Editorial Board (2016) "Donald Trump's Weird World" @ http://www.nytimes.com/interactive/interactive/opinion/editorialboard.html/2016/10/12/.

Opashinov, Mark (1995) "Book Review of Lawrence M. Solan's *The Language of Judges* University of Chicago Press (1993)" 20(2) *Queen's Law Journal*, 641-47

Robertson, Ian (1987) *Sociology* 3rd edition (New York: Worth Publishers).

Rowat, Donald C. (1968) "The Problems of Governing Federal Capitals" 1(3) *Revue canadienne de science politique*, 345-56

Russell, Peter H. (2004) *Constitutional Odyssey: Can Canadians Become a Sovereign People?* 3rd edition (Toronto: University of Toronto Press).

Scassa, T. (1997) "Langue et justice: la transformation du droit" 1(2) *Revue de la Common Law* (), 247.

Shapiro, Evan Joel (1995) *The Supranational Challenge: Federal and Decentralized Unitary States Within the European Union* (LL.M. Thesis, McGill University).

Solan, L.M. (1993) *The Language of Judges* (Chicago: University of Chicago Press).

Stark, Frank M. (1976) "Federalism in Cameroon: The Shadow and the Reality" 10(3) *Canadian Journal of African Studies*, 423-42.

Tremblay, André (1996) "Les droits linguistiques", in G-A. Beaudoin et E.P. Mendes (eds.), *Charte canadienne des droits et libertés* 3e édition (Montréal: Wilson et Lafleur Ltée), 901.

Trent, John E. (1999) "Retaking the 'Middle Ground' – Alliance Candidate Says He Offers English-speakers a Chance to Renew Group's Credibility" *Montreal Gazette* (20 March), B5.

Turpel, Mary Ellen (1991) "Aboriginal Peoples and the Canadian Charter: Interpretive Monopolies, Cultural Differences", in R.F. Devlin (ed.), *Canadian Perspectives on Legal Theory* (Toronto: Emond Montgomery Publications Limited), 503-538.

Washington Post Editorial Board, (2016) "Donald Trump's Strategy for Minority Americans? Don't Let Them Vote" @ https/www.washingtonpost.com/opinions/trumps-strategy-for-minority-americans-don't-let-them-vote/2016/10/11/e3c509-8fe9-11e6.

Will, George F. (2-16) "Donald Trump is the GOP's Chemotherapy" @ https/www.washingtonpost.com/opinions/Donald-trumps-vile-candidacy-is-chemotherapy-for-the-gop/2016/10/10/73e40f30-8f05-11e6.

Williams, Patricia J. 1987. "Alchemical Notes: Reconstructing Ideals from Deconstructed Rights" 22 *Harvard Civil Rights-Civil Liberty Law Review* 401-433.

Mmap Nonfiction and Academic books

If you have enjoyed **BATTLING LANGUAGE RIGHTS GOVERNANCE IN AFRICA: SWISSELGIANISM, UBACKISM, AND THE AMBAZONIA-CAMEROUN WAR**, consider these other fine *Nonfiction and Academic* books from Mwanaka Media and Publishing:

Cultural Hybridity and Fixity by Andrew Nyongesa
Tintinnabulation of Literary Theory by Andrew Nyongesa
South Africa and United Nations Peacekeeping Offensive Operations by Antonio Garcia
A Case of Love and Hate by Chenjerai Mhondera
A Cat and Mouse Affair by Bruno Shora
The Scholarship Girl by Abigail George
The Gods Sleep Through It All by Wonder Guchu
PHENOMENOLOGY OF DECOLONIZING THE UNIVERSITY: Essays in the Contemporary Thoughts of Afrikology by Zvikomborero Kapuya
Africanization and Americanization Anthology Volume 1, Searching for Interracial, Interstitial, Intersectional and Interstates Meeting Spaces, Africa Vs North America by Tendai R Mwanaka
Africa, UK and Ireland: Writing Politics and Knowledge Production Vol 1 by Tendai R Mwanaka
Writing Language, Culture and Development, Africa Vs Asia Vol 1 by Tendai R Mwanaka, Wanjohi wa Makokha and Upal Deb
Zimbolicious: An Anthology of Zimbabwean Literature and Arts, Vol 3 by Tendai Mwanaka
Drawing Without Licence by Tendai R Mwanaka
Writing Grandmothers/ Escribiendo sobre nuestras raíces: Africa Vs Latin America Vol 2 by Tendai R Mwanaka and Felix Rodriguez

Nationalism: (Mis)Understanding Donald Trump's Capitalism, Racism, Global Politics, International Trade and Media Wars, Africa Vs North America Vol 2 by Tendai R Mwanaka

It Is Not About Me: Diaries 2010-2011 by Tendai Rinos Mwanaka

Chitungwiza Mushamukuru: An Anthology from Zimbabwe's Biggest Ghetto Town by Tendai Rinos Mwanaka

The Day and the Dweller: A Study of the Emerald Tablets by Jonathan Thompson

Zimbolicious Anthology Vol 4: An Anthology of Zimbabwean Literature and Arts by Tendai Rinos Mwanaka and Jabulani Mzinyathi

Parks and Recreation by Abigail George

FAMILY LAW AND POLITICS WITH BIOLOGY AND ROYALTY IN AFRICA AND NORTH AMERICA by Peter Ateh-Afec Fossungo

Writing Robotics, Africa Vs Asia, Vol 2 by Tendai Rinos Mwanaka

Zimbolicious Anthology Vol 5: An Anthology of Zimbabwean Literature and Arts by Tendai R. Mwanaka

Love Notes: Everything is Love, An Anthology of Indigenous Languages of Africa and East Europe by Tendai R Mwanaka

Soon to be released

Zimbabwe: Beyond Robert Mugabe by Tendai Rinos Mwanaka

Zimbolicious Anthology Vol 6: An Anthology of Zimbabwean Literature and Arts by Tendai R. Mwanaka and Chenjerai Mhondera

https://facebook.com/MwanakaMediaAndPublishing/

www.ingramcontent.com/pod-product-compliance
Lightning Source LLC
Chambersburg PA
CBHW051616230426
43668CB00013B/2124